W9-DDJ-241

DEFYING CONVENTION
WOMEN WHO CHANGED THE RULES

WOMEN
ENTREPRENEURS

KATHLYN GAY

Enslow Publishing

101 W. 23rd Street
Suite 240
New York, NY 10011
USA

enslow.com

Published in 2017 by Enslow Publishing, LLC.
101 W. 23rd Street, Suite 240, New York, NY 10011

Library of Congress Cataloging-in-Publication Data

Names: Gay, Kathlyn, author.
Title: Women entrepreneurs / Kathlyn Gay.
Description: New York, NY : Enslow Publishing, 2017. | Series: Defying convention:
women who changed the rules | Includes bibliographical references and index.
Identifiers: LCCN 2016021450 | ISBN 9780766081437 (library bound)
Subjects: LCSH: Businesswomen—United States—History—Juvenile literature. |
Women-owned business enterprises—United States—History—Juvenile literature. |
Entrepreneurship—United States—History—Juvenile literature.
Classification: LCC HD6072.6.U5 G39 2017 | DDC 338/.04092520973—dc23
LC record available at https://lccn.loc.gov/2016021450

Printed in Malaysia

To Our Readers: We have done our best to make sure all websites in this book were
active and appropriate when we went to press. However, the author and the publisher
have no control over and assume no liability for the material available on those websites or on any websites they may link to. Any comments or suggestions can be sent by
e-mail to customerservice@enslow.com.

Photo Credits: Cover (top left) Jamie McCarthy/Getty Images; cover (top right), p.
108 Amy Etra/The LIFE Images Collection/Getty Images; cover (bottom left), p. 105
Bloomberg/Getty Images; cover (bottom right), p. 53 ullstein bild/Getty Images; p.
5 Noam Galai/WireImage/Getty Images; p. 13 From The New York Public Library;
p. 16 © Collection of the New-York Historical Society, USA/Bridgeman Images; p.
21 © North Wind Picture Archives; p. 26 Bettmann/Getty Images; p. 30 Schlesinger
Library, Radcliffe Institute, Harvard University/Bridgeman Images; p. 34 Chicago
History Museum/Archive Photos/Getty Images; p. 40 Courtesy National Park
Service, Maggie L. Walker National Historic Site; p. 45 Michael Ochs Archives/Getty
Images; p. 50 Leonard Mccombe/The LIFE Picture Collection/Getty Images; pp. 57,
70 Library of Congress Prints and Photographs Division; p. 58 Cheryl Chenet/Corbis
Historical/Getty Images; p. 63 The United States Patent and Trademark Office; p. 67
digitalreflections/Shutterstock.com; p. 73 Matt Campbell/AFP/Getty Images; p. 79
Photo © PVDE/Bridgeman Images; p. 82 Ed Maker/The Denver Post/Getty Images;
p. 85 Martha Holmes/The LIFE Images Collection/Getty Images; pp. 88, 103 © AP
Images; p. 95 Rose Hartman/Archive Photos/Getty Images; p. 99 Dominique Faget/
AFP/GettyImages

CONTENTS

W omen who have become entrepreneurs — business owners — have a long
history in the United States and worldwide.
They have started and invested in businesses,
often at financial risk and personal hardship.
Before the twentieth century, women were
expected to be housewives and caregivers for
their families. When married women took
jobs outside the home or started businesses,
it was usually a matter of survival — their
families were impoverished and needed the
income. Most single women had no source of
income, except what they could earn at jobs
or in small businesses of their own.

In contrast, many women in current
times are business owners who have made
economic and social impacts on US culture.
In 2015, women owned 30 percent of all US
businesses. Today, many of these women are
highly visible — offering advice, selling their
books, and touting the products or services
offered by their enterprises.

Some of these women — past and present — are profiled in this resource. Their
stories begin in colonial times and during the
American Revolution, proceeding through
US history from the 1600s to the present.
Each chapter explains what was happening
in the nation and abroad when these women
launched their enterprises.

Throughout history, women were not exactly welcomed in the business world. Today, women entrepreneurs are celebrated. Above, a panel of women participates in the United Nations Women's Entrepreneurship Day.

War, economic depressions, and social conflicts have often wreaked havoc. Nevertheless, women have begun businesses with hope and the desire to succeed, even when they faced grueling obstacles. Often, they have pursued businesses that social custom decreed as male-only enterprises.

Women of earlier decades set the stage and paved the way for later female entrepreneurs. Consider these colonial women: Margaret Hardenbroek De Vries Philipse was a merchant and ship owner; Mary Alexander imported goods from England to colonial America; Mary Katherine Goddard was a successful publisher; and Elizabeth "Betsy" Griscom Ross Ashburn Claypoole ran a successful upholstery business. Throughout the 1800s and early 1900s, businesswomen and female inventors included Lydia Pinkham, who developed a medical compound; Martha Coston, who produced naval flares to guide ships; Bertha Palmer, a luxury hotel owner; and Maggie Lena Walker, a bank president. Madame C. J. Walker and Estée Lauder established lucrative cosmetics companies. Helena Rubinstein and Elizabeth Arden created opulent salons and amassed fortunes. And Dame Anita Roddick earned millions of dollars developing bath products made from natural materials.

Adding to this list of successful businesswomen are Ruth Wakefield, creator of the Toll House Cookie, an all-time favorite for millions of people; Olive Beech, an aviation industry executive; Ruth Handler, inventor of the world-famous Barbie doll and her boyfriend, Ken; Brownie Wise, the woman behind Tupperware parties; Joyce Chen, restaurateur and inventor of the flat-bottomed wok; Jean Nidetch, creator of Weight Watcher's formula; and Lillian Vernon, catalog merchant and online retailer.

In contemporary times, successful women entrepreneurs include Diane von Furstenberg, Arianna Huffington, Oprah Winfrey, Weili Dai, Nely Galán, and many others in varied fields of business ownership. All of the women mentioned, along with millions more, have in various ways defied convention and shown that entrepreneurship is not a field restricted entirely to men. It flourishes on inspiration, hope, and perseverance.

CHAPTER ONE

BEFORE AND AFTER THE REVOLUTION

During colonial times in the 1600s, women's roles were often limited. In colonies founded by settlers from England (part of the British Empire), English customs and laws prevailed. Men were dominant and girls and women were expected to be submissive—to obey their fathers, older brothers, and husbands. Females tended to the household—providing childcare, cooking, weaving, cleaning, doing laundry, gardening, and caring for livestock. Few women even thought about starting businesses, although they were expected to contribute their labor in one form or another in a family enterprise. Married women in the English colonies had no legal authority to own land, although widows and unmarried women could buy and sell property.

In spite of being relegated to domestic tasks, colonial women were active in some types of business ventures before the American Revolution. For example, Jane Mecom, younger sister of the colonial printer Benjamin Franklin, built forms to make soap and helped make the product Crown Soap, which the Franklins sold in their store.

Conflicts erupted in the colonies when the British government added one tax after another on various goods shipped to the North American colonies. Colonists staged protests. They argued that the taxes were unfair because they had no voice in the English Parliament.

Women played major roles in defying the British tax system. When the British East India Company added a tax on tea, they assumed women would not refuse to buy their favorite beverage. But they were wrong. Many colonial women responded by boycotting tea—refusing to buy it, and publicly pledging not to do so until England removed the tax.

The tax also prompted a group of colonists to sneak aboard a ship with a cargo of tea anchored in Boston Harbor. Colonists disguised as indigenous people dumped hundreds of cases of tea into the bay. The action became known as the Boston Tea Party. Every region had its own dissidents and revolutionaries, called Rebels or Patriots. Other colonists, known as Loyalists or Tories, were dedicated to the King of England.

During the Revolutionary War (1775–1783), women supported both the Rebel and the Loyalist causes. On the Rebel side, women refused to buy silks and satins and other goods imported from England. Some Patriot women joined the Homespun Movement, weaving their own wool, cotton, or other fabric to make clothing and bedding for their families, and to politically and publicly resist the British. Numerous women worked as cooks or maids for both the American and British armies. In these jobs, they overheard conversations about military maneuvers, information they passed on to commanders. In other words, they became spies for one side or the other. Some women disguised themselves in male clothing and joined armed forces.

After the war and the formation of United States of America, shipping and trade resumed at a rapid pace in manufactured goods, raw materials, and slaves. Slavery was legal in all thirteen colonies. Although trade was sometimes subject to armed conflict and piracy, some businesses made great strides. Women who ran successful businesses before and during this time period include Margaret Philipse, Mary Alexander, Mary Goddard, and Elizabeth Claypoole. They set examples for the generations that followed.

MARGARET HARDENBROECK PHILIPSE (1631?–1690?)

Margaret Hardenbroeck Philipse was a merchant and manager of a successful business in colonial America during the 1600s. She owned ships and sailed back and forth across the Atlantic Ocean, managing her financial affairs.

Margaret was born in about 1631 (sources provide varied dates) in the Rhine Valley of the Netherlands, a part of the German Empire of the time. She was the daughter of Adolph Hardenbroek and his second wife, Maria Katernberg. Little is known about her early life, but Margaret probably received an education as a young child. According to The National Society of Colonial Dames, the Netherlands, "was the only European country in seventeenth-century Europe to provide primary education to females."[1] People of the Netherlands, called the Dutch, also believed in women's rights, and carried this belief with them over to North America. Margaret Hardenbroek immigrated in 1659 to the Dutch colony called New Amsterdam, which later became New York. A wealthy cousin, Wolter Valck, offered Margaret a job managing his businesses and selling merchandise for a commission.

The Dutch were strong believers in equality. Women in the Dutch society of New Amsterdam had more independence than those in other colonies, including the freedom to work outside the home. In the colony's business world, Margaret was known as a she-agent. She traded a variety of goods and sold merchandise to the Netherlands.

When she was twenty-eight years old, Margaret married Pieter DeVries, a wealthy widow and merchant-trader who was twice Margaret's age. Author Jean Zimmerman explains that it was not unusual for widowers and widows to remarry quickly. Colonial life was full of risks—epidemics, shipwrecks, conflicts between settlers and indigenous peoples, and other daily hazards—so "there was no advantage to a long engagement."[2]

Pieter and Margaret DeVries had a daughter, Maria, in 1660. That same year, Pieter DeVries died. He left a large estate, including a shipping and trading business, which Margaret took over and expanded. In 1663, Margaret remarried. Her second husband was Frederick Philipse, a prominent member of New Amsterdam's social and business life. The Philipse estate was vast, with mansions, farm buildings, and animals on more than 50,000 acres along the Hudson River.

The Philipse family included five children: Maria (renamed Eva when Frederick adopted her), the couple's three sons, and a daughter. While she

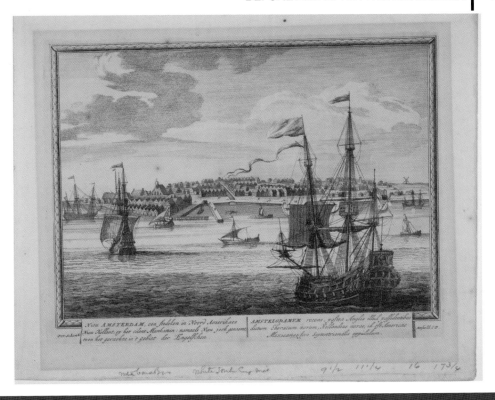

The Dutch colony of New Amsterdam operated on principles of equality quite different from other American colonies. Here, Margaret Hardenbroeck Philipse was free to become a lucrative trader.

was raising a family, Margaret traveled across the Atlantic Ocean to oversee her trading activities. At times, one of her children sailed with her.

When Margaret married, Dutch law allowed her to maintain control of her finances and her trading business, as well as her ships — the *New Netherland Indian, Beaver, Pearl,* and *Morning Star*. But when the British, who often fought the Dutch, seized New Amsterdam in 1664, they

renamed it the Province of New York. Under
British rule, Margaret had to forfeit most of her
rights. According to British law, she could no
longer be independent, and all of her businesses
and her earnings would belong to her husband.
Nevertheless, Margaret Hardenbroeck Philipse
continued to operate the trading and shipping
enterprises. The businesses prospered and the couple gained great wealth.

In 1680, Margaret retired, and her sons managed her businesses. She died circa 1691. "Although
she was helped early on by an inheritance from
her first husband, her achievements were almost
exclusively hers. She was an extraordinary businesswoman," wrote Maggie MacLean.[3] In fact,
numerous authors writing about colonial America
have included the accomplishments of entrepreneur Margaret Hardenbroeck Philipse in their
books. Thus, Margaret's example for other businesswomen lives on.

MARY SPRATT PROVOOST ALEXANDER (1693–1760)

Another important colonial entrepreneur of Dutch
heritage was Mary Spratt Provoost Alexander. She
imported goods from Europe to colonial America.
Mary Spratt was born April 17, 1693, the daughter

of New York residents John and Maria Jans de Peyster Spratt. Information about Mary's early life is sparse, although the research database at American History Online explains that her father died in 1697 "and her mother married the smuggler David Provoost, whose surname the Spratt children adopted. Three years later Maria Provoost died, and [Mary] moved into her maternal grandmother's home."[4]

In 1711, Mary married Samuel Provoost, her stepfather's younger brother and a successful importer of dry goods and fabrics. Mary Provoost invested the money that she had received from her mother's estate into her husband's business; she also became his financial partner. The couple had three children—John, David, and Maria.

When Samuel died in about 1720, Maria Provoost assumed control of the import enterprise, which prospered. Ships docking in New York City usually had a large order of goods, such as expensive silks, wools, lace, and crepe, for the Provoost business.

In 1721 Mary Provoost married a prominent New York lawyer and politician, John Alexander. The Alexanders were the parents of seven children—sons, William and James; and daughters, Mary, Elizabeth, Catherine, Anna, and Susannah. Smallpox took the lives of James in 1731 and Anna in 1746.

Mary Spratt Provoost Alexander was one of colonial New York City's most successful importers.

The large Alexander household would have occupied most women's time and efforts. However, Mary and her husband were wealthy, and lived in a mansion on Broad Street in New York City. They no doubt had servants to help care for the children and household needs.

Nevertheless, Mary directed the care of her children, and also supported her husband's political and business career. At the same time, she managed her import enterprise. She sold imported fabrics, regular dry goods, and Indian blankets, as well as fine china, glassware, silver and other luxury items in her store, the Emporium. The store was built in front of the Alexander mansion. In fact, just hours after the birth of her first daughter, Mary Alexander was back in the Emporium, selling merchandise.[5]

John Alexander died in 1756, and Mary continued the import business. She amassed a fortune, and her mansion became "a meeting place for politicians and business people…With her social connections and her successful business, Mary was a prominent member of colonial society and is reputed to have served as an informal advisor to many New York politicians."[6] In fact, she became one of the wealthiest women in New York. She died of pleurisy on April 18, 1760, leaving not only a financial legacy, but also a historical example for other women hoping to succeed in business.

MARY KATHERINE GODDARD (1738–1816)

Freedom of speech, which includes freedom of the press, was a consistent part of Mary Katherine Goddard's life. Belief in that freedom remained steady before and after the Revolutionary War, and was influential in her decision to become the publisher of a rebel newspaper.

Mary Katherine was born on June 16, 1738, in New London, Connecticut. Her parents, Dr. Giles and Sarah Updike Goddard, were well educated, as were their two children, Mary and her younger brother, William. Dr. Goddard was the postmaster of New London, Connecticut, and the whole family was involved with the postal system during most of their lives.

Mary's brother, William, was an apprentice in the printing trade. When Dr. Goddard died in 1762, Sarah Goddard helped her son, then aged twenty-two, to set up a printing shop in Providence, Rhode Island. Mary and her mother both worked at the shop, beginning Mary Katherine's publishing career. Mary never married, and became an indispensable figure in the Goddard printing business. The Goddards published the weekly *Providence Gazette* until the end of 1768.

In the meantime, William Goddard had set up another printing shop in Philadelphia, where he published the *Pennsylvania Chronicle*. Mary Katherine joined her brother in that publishing shop, one of the largest in the colonies. William Goddard traveled extensively to promote his printing business. He also dabbled in politics, which soon became his major interest. According to the National Women's History Museum, "After Sarah Goddard's 1770 death, Mary Katherine kept the business running, as William was frequently jailed for public outbursts and rabble-rousing articles in the paper."[7]

Although she did not legally share ownership, Mary Katherine managed the business and kept it operating when her brother left once again for Baltimore in 1773. There he began Baltimore's first newspaper, the *Maryland Journal*. The Philadelphia shop closed in 1774, and Mary Katherine moved to Baltimore to oversee the new plant and newspaper, eventually becoming its sole publisher.

Through William's political connections, Mary Katherine also became Baltimore's postmistress. The postal service helped distribute the rebel newspaper throughout the colony.

At the beginning of the Revolutionary War, Britain refused to export paper stock to the colonies in an attempt to stop rebel newspapers. But Goddard did not give up. She set up her own paper mill. At the time, paper was made from rags, and when the price of rags increased rapidly, Goddard was forced to buy low-quality paper. She wrote:

> "[The] enormous prices demanded at the Stores here for Paper, constrains us to print the MARYLAND JOURNAL on this dark and poor sort" [of paper].[8]

Her publishing business eventually obtained better stock, and printed the first copy of the Declaration of Independence that included names of all the signers.

ELIZABETH "BETSY" GRISCOM ROSS ASHBURN CLAYPOOLE (1752–1836)

Most people who have read American history know her as Betsy Ross. Legend says she made the first American flag. But historians have not validated the flag story because facts are scarce. As Ed Crews noted in the *Colonial Williamsburg Journal*, "Ross is so beloved and so deeply embedded in the nation's memory that somehow it seems unpatriotic, if not vaguely treasonous, to cast doubt on her story. The truth, however, is that nobody can prove that Betsy Ross had anything to do with the first official Stars and Stripes."[9] Regardless, Betsy Ross established herself as a flag maker and an important businesswoman before and after the Revolutionary War.

Elizabeth "Betsy" Griscom was born on January 1, 1752 in Philadelphia, Pennsylvania, to Samuel and Rebecca James Griscom. Her parents were members of the Religious Society of Friends, known as Friends or Quakers, and were pacifists. Elizabeth attended Quaker schools, where she learned needlework, an acceptable occupation for a woman of that time. In fact, her father arranged for her to be an apprentice in upholstery, which required expert sewing skills.

When she was in her early twenties, Elizabeth married John Ross. He was a member of the Episcopal Christ Church, which George Washington often attended. Because of her marriage to a non-Quaker, Elizabeth Ross was expelled from the Friends. She eventually joined the Free Quakers, who were a bit more liberal.

The woman we know as Betsy Ross may or may not have sewn the first American flag, but she did run a successful flagmaking and upholstery businesss in Philadelphia.

After their marriage, John and Elizabeth opened their own upholstery business. Part of the venture was making flags, a common practice in upholstering enterprises. It was the beginning of the Revolutionary War, however, and fabrics were not readily available, hampering the Ross's business. John then joined the Pennsylvania militia. He was guarding an ammunition supply when it exploded, seriously wounding him. He died in mid-January 1776.

Elizabeth "Betsy" Ross kept the business going and made flags for Pennsylvania ships. She married again in 1777. Betsy and her second husband, Joseph Ashburn, had two daughters, one of whom died in her youth. Ashburn, a sea captain, sailed to the West Indies to obtain war supplies for the Revolution. He was captured by the English and was sent to Old Mill Prison in England, where he died in March 1782.

Betsy soon married her third husband, John Claypoole. He had been imprisoned with Ashburn and was a family friend. The couple had five daughters. Claypoole lived for many years, but was sickly. He died in 1817 after a long illness. With her daughters, Betsy continued to sew upholstery and make flags and banners for the new states. She retired from the business in about 1826, and died in 1836.

In 1870, one of Betsy's grandsons told how the flag-making story originated. He admitted that he could not confirm that Betsy Ross made the first American flag. He based his anecdotal account on his memory of Ross, who lived in his home when he was eleven years old. His story was published in *Harper's Monthly* in 1873, and during the next decade, the legend was included in many school textbooks. The story has often overshadowed the accounts of Elizabeth Griscom Ross Ashburn Claypoole's business success. However, her achievements both as an entrepreneur, and as a homemaker and mother, are now published online and elsewhere.

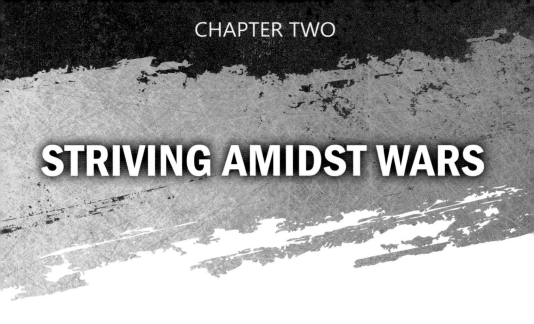

CHAPTER TWO

STRIVING AMIDST WARS

After the Revolutionary War ended in 1783, the new nation faced numerous challenges. Between 1784 and 1789, they faced a major economic depression, for example. The prices of many goods that had been inflated during the war, fell. Veterans did not receive their pensions. Business people, farmers, and other landowners could not pay off debts. Some ended up in debtors' prisons, modeled after those in London. An 1883 law abolished this practice, and much later, it was found unconstitutional. But many people even today have been and are jailed simply because they are too poor to pay a fine or debt.

In spite of financial problems, some businesses and industries succeeded. One such business was the Lukens' boilerplate factory, which Rebecca Lukens (1794-1854) managed after her husband, Charles, died. The company was almost bankrupt, but Lukens built an enterprise, soon becoming the leading manufacturer of boilerplates for iron-hulled ships.

UNEASY PEACE

In the 1800s, peace rarely prevailed. There were economic and political uprisings and armed conflicts. The new nation was expanding, violently displacing indigenous people from their lands. There were also increasing hostilities with Britain. Many Americans called for another battle with Great Britain, and war ensued from 1812 to 1815. As in the Revolution, women disguised themselves and joined soldiers in the battlefield.

After the War of 1812, construction on the Erie Canal began. This new transportation system began in New York, and linked Lake Erie to the other Great Lakes, as well as to the Northwest Territory. The canal system allowed people to move inland, developing farms and towns. Farmers could ship their produce to eastern cities, while manufacturers and businesses could ship their goods west. Along with the canal system, railroads and roads were built, allowing an increasing number of people to move into the Midwest. Farms, towns, and cities developed. Factories on the east coast, such as textile mills, produced fabrics, yarns, and clothes that were sent inland.

WOMEN IN TEXTILE INDUSTRIES

Beginning in the 1820s, New England textile factories hired many girls and women who worked long hours spinning and weaving for low wages. At first, some women in the mills seemed to like their work. Adeline Cowles of Hartford, Connecticut, was employed in a factory in Lowell, Massachusetts, in 1847. In a letter to her sister, she wrote:

> I arived here safely, and have gone to work in the Spining room. I like it very much indeed it is very easy pretty work after you once get lerned, but it requires some patience to lern when you first begin. I almost gave up in despair the first day, it made my fingers so sore, but I thought if the other girls could lern I could and now the work seames quite easy to me.[1]

Nevertheless, numerous women soon found factory employment oppressive. Female workers lived in boarding houses near the factories, six to a room. Rules strictly regulated their lives, from early rising at 5:00 a.m., to the end of their twelve-hour workday at 7:00 p.m., to curfew at 10:00 p.m. During the 1840s and 1850s, women began to join the Ten Hour Movement, engaging in protests to demand the reduction of the workday to ten hours. They also advocated for an increase in wages, and safer working conditions.

The advent of the Industrial Revolution changed working roles for both women and men. Suddenly, work moved out of the home and into the factory. Women often found jobs at textile mills, and with that came a sliver of independence.

Some mill women also got involved in other reform movements. According to Professor Thomas Duncan of State University of New York, "Anti-slavery was strong in Lowell and mill women sent several petitions to Washington opposing slavery in the District of Columbia … Woman reformers came to see opposition to black slavery and wage slavery as related causes. Some also participated in the women's rights conventions that mushroomed after the first one was held in Seneca Falls, New York, in July 1848."[2]

As industrialization and calls for reforms expanded, so did the idea of "Manifest Destiny." Manifest Destiny was a belief that Americans had the divine right to possess the entire continent, and to claim its resources, regardless of the consequences for the indigenous peoples already inhabiting the land. During the 1800s, people pushed even farther into the continent's interior. Some were intent on mining for gold in the West, creating what was known as "gold fever."

MORE FIGHTING

With all the growth, there was still more violence, as colonizers sought to wrest land from indigenous peoples. War also erupted with Mexico, a huge nation that included the land now encompassed by Arizona, California, New Mexico, Nevada, Utah, and sections of Colorado. Texas, too, had once been part of Mexico, but had declared independence in 1836. Mexico would not accept the independence of the Republic of Texas, and the United States also wanted to annex it. This conflict led to war between the United States and Mexico. The war began in 1846 and ended in 1848, when the United States claimed victory and the state of Texas as its own.

As is well known, the major war of the 1800s was the Civil War (1861-1865), which divided the country between the Northern and Western regions, and the Southern confederation of states that sought to secede from the Union. Although Americans today often debate the causes of the war, the two sides primarily fought over whether or not slavery would be abolished. Tens of thousands died or were severely injured in the many clashes.

In spite of all the warfare during the 1800s, US women continued to advocate for social, economic, and labor reforms, women's rights, and the abolition of slavery. Throughout the 1800s, and into the early 1900s, businesswomen such as Lydia Pinkham, Martha Coston, Bertha Palmer, and Maggie Walker attended to their enterprises.

LYDIA ESTES PINKHAM (1819–1883)

Lydia Pinkham developed and sold a home remedy, Lydia E. Pinkham's Vegetable Compound, which was known by her name. A modified version of that health tonic is still on store shelves today under that name.

Lydia Estes Pinkham was the daughter of William and Rebecca Chase Estes. She was born in 1819 in Lynn, Massachusetts. Lydia was homeschooled during her early years, and later attended Lynn Academy. Her parents were Quakers and their home was often a gathering place for abolitionists. However, the Estes family left the Friends because of a conflict over slavery. While they were fighting for the abolition of slavery, some other Quakers continued to be slave traders during colonial times. The Estes joined the Universalists denomination.

As a teenager, Lydia, with her family, was involved in various social causes and was a strong anti-slavery advocate. She was a member of the Lynn Female Anti-Slavery Society and knew activists such as Frederick Douglass, who was a neighbor and a family friend throughout her life. During her early twenties, Lydia worked as a schoolteacher and nurse. In 1843, she married a widower, Isaac Pinkham, who invested, off and on, in several different enterprises.

Lydia became a typical homemaker and mother. The family included the couple's five children, one of whom died, and Isaac's five-year-old daughter from his previous marriage. As was common in most households, Lydia was responsible for maintaining the family's health, and she made a tonic of herbs, roots, and alcohol to treat a variety of ailments. She also shared the mixture with neighbors and friends.

A worldwide economic depression wreaked havoc in North America and Europe from October 1873 to March 1879. Like numerous Americans, the Estes family suffered financial losses, and by 1875, Isaac was bankrupt. He was so distressed that he became ill and was unable to work.

With the family impoverished, Lydia Pinkham began selling her home remedy. She set up a factory in her basement and her children helped supply bottles for her tonic, which they sold door-to-door. In 1876, she began advertising her product in newspapers, and sales increased. When Pinkham added her photograph to ads in 1879, her healthy, grandmotherly image improved sales so much that she received profitable offers to trademark the product. But she refused and continued to sell Lydia E. Pinkham's Vegetable Compound herself.

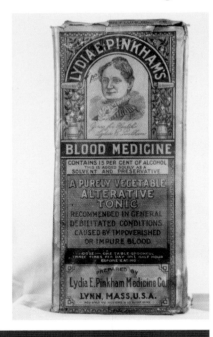

Lydia Pinkham's vegetable tonic was said to treat a variety of ailments.

Women were the primary customers for the tonic, which they took for "women's problems." Most girls and women in the 1800s found it embarrassing to discuss painful menstruation or other problems with male doctors.

Pinkham created a formula for compounds to treat a wide variety of illnesses. She was unable to cure her two sons, however, when they became ill with tuberculosis. At the time, there was no effective treatment, and both died in 1881. Pinkham's daughter and surviving son helped her carry on. After Pinkham had a stroke in 1882, she was paralyzed, and a year later, she died.

Lydia Pinkham's son, Charles, took over the business. In 1968, due to family disagreements and the new federal regulations on medicinal products, the Pinkhams sold the company. Almost two decades later, Numark Laboratories obtained a license for the medicine. It still sells today in tablet or pill form in supermarkets and various pharmacies; it is also available for sale online. Clearly, the product has a long legacy. But it would not even exist if not for Lydia E. Pinkham's concern for women's health, and her ability to defy convention and become a successful entrepreneur. She was a forerunner of today's wellness campaigns.

MARTHA JANE HUNT COSTON (1826–1904)

Martha Coston developed a signal system for ships. She patented the system and became a highly successful businesswoman.

She was born Martha Jane Hunt in 1826 in Baltimore, Maryland. In the 1830s, Martha's widowed mother moved young Martha and her older sisters and brothers to Philadelphia, Pennsylvania. Little has been written about her early childhood, but in her autobiography, Martha wrote:

> The years slipped rapidly and happily away, and found
> me at fourteen unusually tall and mature in appearance
> for my age ... I went to school and studied with ardor,
> spending my evenings with my mother in her quiet
> sitting-room getting ready my lessons for the next day,
> while my two sisters entertained their young friends
> and beaux in the drawing-room.[3]

Martha soon had her own "beaux," or boyfriend, nineteen-year-old Benjamin Coston. Even
as a teenager, he was a skilled inventor. Benjamin
courted Martha for several years. He promised her
mother that the two would not marry until Martha
was eighteen.

Benjamin's expertise as a nautical inventor
caught the attention of the US Secretary of the
Navy, who offered Coston a position overseeing a
scientific expedition at sea. Benjamin and Martha
feared they would be separated for a long time, so
they decided to elope. At sixteen, Martha became a
wife, and her twenty-one-year-old husband was on
his way to the Navy Yard.

For several years, the Costons made their
home in Washington, DC, and then moved
to Boston, Massachusetts. There, Benjamin
went to work for the Boston Gas Company.
The family included four sons. But tragedy hit
when Benjamin died unexpectedly at the age of

twenty-six. His death was blamed on exposure to numerous toxic chemicals used in his inventions.

Martha and her boys returned to Philadelphia to live with her mother. Shortly thereafter, both Coston's youngest son and her mother passed away. Adding to her grief was the fact that she had limited funds. She had to find a way to earn income.

She leafed through her husband's notebooks, looking for inventions that could be produced. "At last I came upon a large envelope containing papers and a skillfully drawn plan of signals to be used at sea, at night, for the same purpose of communication that flags are used by day," Martha wrote. "This chart was colored and showed that to each signal was attached a number and letter."[4]

For several years, Coston experimented with the flares, and in 1859, developed a system that used color cartridges fired from a pistol. Various combinations of white, red, and green correspond to numbers, and relay messages such as "enemy to our left," or "send troops to our right."[5] After much testing and hassle, the US Navy bought the patent for Pyrotechnic Night Signals in 1861 at the start of the Civil War. The Navy paid Coston $20,000, half of what she had requested, and used the flares extensively during the war.

Coston also secured patents for her invention in a number of European countries. "After the Civil War, the Coston Signal continued in widespread use by many foreign governments, commercial merchants, private yachting clubs, and most significantly by the US Life Saving Service," wrote Denise E. Pilato of Eastern Michigan University. Pilato concluded: "It is not only her accomplishments as a businesswoman and inventor that present a fascinating portrait ... Martha J. Coston's signal and story may indeed still function as a signal to the world, one that communicates the contributions of many professional women inventors that followed in her path."[6] Coston died in 1904, but the Coston Signal Company remained in business until about 1985.

BERTHA MATILDE HONORÉ PALMER (1849–1918)

She lived in luxury, and could have savored her privileged position, doing little to impact American social and economic concerns. Instead, Bertha Matilde Honoré became a successful entrepreneur as well as an advocate for working people, especially women.

Bertha Matilde was born on May 22, 1849, in Louisville,

After the Great Chicago Fire destroyed most of her husband's holdings, capable Bertha Palmer helped him rebuild his fortune.

Kentucky. She was the second child of successful businessman Henri (Henry) Honoré, and his wife, Eliza Carr Honoré. The upper-class, southern family, which included six children, moved in 1855 to Chicago, where Henry invested in real estate and added to his wealth.

Bertha was privately educated in Catholic schools and excelled in her studies. She also learned about business and real estate from her father. When she was thirteen, she met a business associate of her father, Potter Palmer. Palmer owned a dry-goods store that eventually became Marshall Field's, and later became a real estate tycoon and builder of a luxury hotel, the Palmer House.

Potter Palmer, who was twice Martha's age, was attracted to the teenager, but waited until Bertha was older to court her. The two were married in 1870. He was forty-four, and she was twenty-one. The wedding present for Mrs. Palmer was the Palmer House Hotel, which was under construction and almost complete. For their honeymoon, the couple traveled to England and part of Europe, visiting castles, museums, and art galleries, attending concerts, meeting with wealthy Americans, and shopping for whatever finery Bertha wanted.

In October of 1871, after a dry summer, fire broke out in a barn behind a home in Chicago. Although the cause of the fire has long been debated, flames quickly spread to other wooden buildings, destroying houses, mansions, stores, restaurants, and industrial buildings. The fire left most of the Palmer real estate holdings, including the hotel, in ashes.

Bertha Palmer immediately contacted lenders so that her husband could re-establish credit and borrow money to rebuild. The new Palmer House was constructed with fireproof materials, and the Palmers moved into a suite in the hotel. After reconstruction, Bertha Palmer became the "queen bee" of Chicago society. By 1885, bedecked in expensive jewelry, she was entertaining in a lavish, forty-two-room mansion on North Lake Shore Drive, the "gold coast" for wealthy Chicagoans. The mansion was filled with paintings and other art collected on trips abroad.

Beyond the glamor and glitter, Bertha Palmer held meetings in her home with groups championing women's rights and trade unions. She also donated to numerous charities. In 1891, she became President of the Board of Lady Managers in preparation for the upcoming World Columbian Exposition, which was to be held in Chicago. When the Exposition, also known as the Chicago World's Fair, opened in 1893, Bertha Palmer entertained royalty and presidents.

After her husband died in 1902, Bertha Palmer began traveling to Florida in the winter, a common practice for northerners today. She not only enjoyed the warm climate, but also the investment opportunities. From 1910 to about 1919, she bought tens of thousands of acres of land on Florida's west coast in Manatee County, part of which became Sarasota County. She developed cattle ranches and "devoted herself to purchasing and improving her acreage, selecting livestock, hiring foremen, [and] overseeing the work force." According to the Sarasota County Government, "She attended to every acre and within each boundary; every structure, waterway, creature and yield. There was not an order written or a contract signed without her express approval. Whether on site or thousands of miles away, she supervised each detail of her domain."[7] Palmer studied numerous agricultural methods, and encouraged others to engage in citrus, dairy, and farming endeavors, as well as cattle ranching in Florida.

In 1916, Palmer was diagnosed with breast cancer. She died at her winter residence in Osprey, Florida, in 1918, and was buried at Graceland Cemetery in Chicago. Her sons, father, and brothers continued to develop her enormous land holdings. The Palmer name adorns streets and buildings in Sarasota, reminding residents and visitors of Bertha Palmer's legacy as an astute entrepreneur.

MAGGIE LENA DRAPER WALKER (1864?–1934)

Maggie Walker was the first black woman to found a bank and be its president. She gained national recognition for her business expertise, as well as her lifelong commitment to a fraternal order benefiting African Americans. She also founded a newspaper whose purpose was to inform the black community about racial injustices in the post-Civil War period.

Maggie Lena was born in 1864 to Elizabeth Draper, a former slave who was a cook for Elizabeth Van Lew, an abolitionist. Maggie's biological father was Eccles Cuthbert, an Irish American who met Elizabeth on the Van Lew estate in Richmond, Virginia. Cuthbert moved on, and Maggie's mother married William Mitchell, a butler on the estate. They had a child, Johnnie, Maggie's half-brother.

In 1876, William Mitchell drowned under mysterious circumstances. Some speculate that he may have been murdered. Although the Mitchell family lived in their own home off the estate, Elizabeth had no income after her husband's death. She decided to start a laundry, one of the few types of business black people of the time were permitted to pursue. After school, young Maggie delivered clean laundry to white customers.

Maggie attended Richmond Colored Normal School. After graduation in 1883, she became a teacher. Three years later, however, she had to quit her job when she married Armstead Walker Jr. because the school disapproved of married women working outside the home. The Walkers had three sons—Russell, Armstead, and Melvin, though

Armstead died in infancy. They also adopted a daughter, Polly Anderson.

While attending Normal, Maggie joined the Independent Order of St. Luke (IOSL), an organization that helped African Americans financially and socially. At first, it was a burial society. Then IOSL became an insurance company to provide benefits for African Americans who could not obtain coverage from discriminatory white companies. At IOSL, Maggie held several offices and led membership drives that brought in tens of thousands of members in about two dozen states. In *Contemporary Black Biography*, James Manheim writes, "Well ahead of her time, she urged black consumers to patronize black-owned businesses, and both personally and professionally campaigned for the equality of the sexes and the economic enfranchisement of women."[8]

In 1902, Walker established a weekly newspaper, *The St. Luke Herald*, to promote closer communication between the IOSL and the public. A year later, she helped open and became president of the St. Luke Penny Savings Bank in Richmond. The bank provided loans to African Americans so that they could buy homes.

In 1915, Maggie's husband was killed in an accident, and she had to manage her household, work, and investments by herself. Over the years, under Walker's leadership, St. Luke acquired other

Maggie Lena Walker founded a bank and championed African American–owned businesses.

black-owned banks, and in 1929, became the Consolidated Bank and Trust Company. She served as chairman of the bank's board. In addition, she was active in numerous organizations advocating for African Americans. She co-founded the Richmond branch of the National Association for the Advancement of Colored People (NAACP).

Walker remained active in civic affairs until her health declined and she was confined to a wheelchair. Nevertheless, she continued as chairman of the bank, and as Right Worthy Grand Secretary of the Independent Order of St. Luke — the top leadership position.

Maggie Lena Walker died on December 15, 1934. To honor her legacy, the US National Park Service purchased the Walker family home, and designated Maggie Walker's community of Jackson Ward as a National Historic Landmark District, which "continues to exemplify the success of African American entrepreneurship," states the National Park Service.[9]

CHAPTER THREE

WOMEN IN BEAUTY AND FASHION BUSINESSES

A fter the Civil War and well into the 1900s, the United States saw continued industrial expansion. As in earlier times, men dominated most enterprises. Numerous women, however, founded successful businesses that appealed primarily to women—such as cosmetic, hair, and fashion companies. Their success came in spite of the fact that cosmetics and stylish apparel were not top priorities when the nation became involved in still more wars: the Spanish-American War in 1898, in which the US intervened to support Cuban revolts against Spanish colonizers, and World War I (1915-1918), which Americans entered into in 1917.

A major economic collapse occurred in 1929, and the Great Depression devastated families across the United States. Many workers lost their jobs and homes. They became nomads, wandering from place to place, trying to find work. By

1933, nearly eleven thousand banks had failed, destroying people's savings, and twelve million Americans were unemployed. For their survival, the unemployed and their families had to depend on soup kitchens for food and various aid centers for clothing.

When President Franklin Delano Roosevelt took office in 1933, he established US government programs such as the Works Progress Administration (WPA), which "employed more than 8.5 million people."[1] Most of the jobs, however, went to men. They built numerous bridges, roads, public buildings, national parks, and airports that still exist. Only 13.5 percent of WPA employees were women, who were consigned to jobs like "sewing, bookbinding, caring for the elderly, school lunch programs, nursery school, and recreational work," according to PBS's *American Experience*.[2]

By the mid 1900s, Americans were once again at war, entering World War II in 1941, when Japan attacked the US naval fleet at Pearl Harbor, Hawaii. As men enlisted for the war, women were needed for military industrial jobs that had traditionally been male-dominated. In fact, "between 1940 and 1945, the female percentage of the US workforce increased from 27 percent to nearly 37 percent, and by 1945, nearly one out of every four married women worked outside the home."[3]

After the war, the US economy recovered, but

men returning from battlefields often replaced women who had been working in wartime industries. By the 1950s, most women were yet again relegated to caring for the home, or to their gendered jobs as secretaries, bank tellers, sales clerks, private household workers, waitresses, or assembly line workers in factories. Many also worked in teaching and nursing professions.

From the late 1800s to the mid 1900s, some women disregarded the norm, and launched businesses that were socially and economically accessible and successful. But as the Smithsonian Institution reported, "[M]ost of these enterprises still fell within ... the women's sphere. Many of these firms concentrated on making and selling products for the home or for personal beautification."[4]

THE BUSINESS OF BEAUTY

The beauty business is hardly new. "Every human society from at least the ancient Egyptians onwards has used beauty products and artifacts to enhance attractiveness," writes history professor Geoffrey Jones, author of *Beauty Imagined: A History of the Global Beauty Industry*.[5] In an interview posted online, Jones explains that ancient Egyptian women adorned their faces and hair. They used eyeliner and blackened their eyelashes, applied face cream, perfume oils, hair colors, and lipsticks. Some of the substances contained lead, copper, and other toxic materials, but little was known about their poisonous effects. Like facial cosmetics, hair adornments and styles also date from ancient times. Egyptians curled their hair with metal tongs. They used animal fat or vegetable oils as a salve for their hair and to form it into elaborate styles. Braids and hair extensions were also common.

Fast-forward many centuries to life in the United States, and you will find similar examples of hair styling. In the early days of the Union, however, some US religious leaders raised objections to cosmetics and other beauty treatments. Women were expected to be "proper" and not to call attention to themselves with adornments. Women who wore makeup were called "hellish" and likened to "Jezebels" who led men astray.

By the middle of the 1800s, however, the Industrial Revolution and advances in chemistry propelled the production and use of various cosmetic products. And the early 1900s saw the beginning of the modern cosmetic and fashion industries. In the 1920s, for example, Paris designer Coco Chanel introduced the "little black dress," business suits, and "flapper dresses" with fringe at the hem. Her enterprise brought her fame and fortune.

In the cosmetic industry, advertisers promoted

the advantages of face creams, makeup, and hair care, which helped to increase the number of consumers and to lower prices. Facial powders, lipsticks, and eye makeup were popular with the female population. So were hair care products and services. Women who recognized the opportunities for beauty and fashion enterprises included Madam C. J. Walker, Helena Rubenstein, Elizabeth Arden, Estee Lauder, and Anita Roddick.

MADAM C. J. WALKER (1867–1919)

Her name has long been associated with hair care products and with her million-dollar business, Madame C. J. Walker Manufacturing Company. But she began her life under quite different circumstances. She was born Sarah Breedlove on December 23, 1867, near Delta, Louisiana. Her parents, Owen and Minerva Anderson Breedlove, were sharecroppers and former slaves.

Sarah "Madam C. J." Walker created a lucrative hair care empire that still exists today.

When Sarah was seven years old, she and her siblings were orphaned. She worked in the cotton fields of Delta and lived in the household of a brother-in-law, who was abusive. At the age of fourteen, she escaped the mistreatment by marrying Moses McWilliams. They had one daughter, Lelia, who was later named A'Lelia. McWilliams died from unknown causes and Sarah had to find a way to make a living. She moved to St. Louis, Missouri, where her brothers were barbers. Sarah found work as a laundress and cook. Earning only $1.50 per day, she was determined that Lelia get an education—which she did.

In 1894, Sarah married John Davis, who proved to be untrustworthy. Sarah felt trapped; she did not want to remain a laundress for the rest of her life. But there were few opportunities open to her. Genealogist and African-American history scholar Henry Louis Gates Jr. explained that black people "in turn-of-the-century America were excluded from most trade unions and denied bank capital, resulting in trapped lives as sharecroppers or menial, low-wage earners. One of the only ways out ... was to start a business ... Hair care and cosmetics fit the bill." Gates added that "Sarah's personal and professional fortune began to turn when she discovered 'The Great Wonderful Hair Grower' of Annie Turnbo (later Malone), an Illinois native with a background in chemistry who'd relocated her hair-straightening business to St. Louis."[6]

In 1904, because of hair loss, Sarah tried Turnbo's product. "Black women's hair loss was commonplace in those days, given the fact that many, if not most, African Americans were badly nourished and lived in conditions of poor hygiene and constant labor," wrote Martha Lagase at Harvard Business School.[7] The Hair Grower worked so well that Sarah became a Turnbo sales agent. At that time, she also met and began dating Charles Joseph (C. J.) Walker, a newspaperman.

Sarah moved to Denver, Colorado, in 1906. That same year, she and C. J. married and she officially became Madam C. J. Walker. They established a company and Madam Walker created a compound that she called Madam Walker's Wonderful Hair Grower. Although the name was similar to Turnbo's product, Walker argued that her formula was her own, and that it was made of natural ingredients.

The Walkers sold their product wherever African Americans gathered, especially in black churches. They also advertised it in black newspapers. To increase sales, Madam Walker encouraged her satisfied customers to become agents. The Walker enterprise expanded rapidly, and by 2010, she had moved her company to Indianapolis, Indiana, a major transportation center at the time.

The business included schools that trained beauticians. The company not only produced the Hair Grower, but also salves, a shampoo, and a hair dressing called Glossine.

The Walkers divorced in 1912, but Madam Walker continued to promote and grow the business, expanding to Latin America and the Caribbean. She returned to the United States and lived in a New York mansion. She continued to oversee the Indianapolis factory and to work in the company's New York office. She was also active in social and political life and shared her wealth with numerous charities such as the NAACP and anti-lynching campaigns.

In 1919, Madam Walker died at her estate, Villa Lewaro, in Irvington-on-Hudson. Four generations of Walker women continued the Madam C. J. Walker Manufacturing Company until it was sold in 1985. The story of Walker's success endures. She has been and still is an inspiration to aspiring entrepreneurs of all races.

HELENA RUBINSTEIN (1870?–1965)

Helena Rubinstein developed a global cosmetic enterprise that thrived even during the Great Depression. She opened luxurious beauty salons in major cities around the world.

Helena was born on December 25, 1870, as her gravestone says, or 1872, as her birth record contends, in Krakow, Poland.[8] Helena's given name was Chaja. She was the first child of Orthodox Jewish parents, Horace and Augusta Rubinstein, who eventually had seven more daughters. Augusta "insisted her daughters would gain influence and power through beauty and love. In fact, Helena Rubinstein's beauty industry began with jars of Modjeska cream, named after her mother's friend, actor Helena Modjeska," according to *Jewish Women's Archive*.[9]

Chaja's father sent her to medical school in Switzerland. She liked the laboratory work but not the hospital duties. She wanted to quit. Her strict father demanded that she finish her education or marry a wealthy widower. Instead, she made her own choice for a husband, who did not suit her parents. She decided to leave Poland and go to Australia to live with an aunt and uncle in western Victoria. She took along twelve jars of her mother's face cream.

After disagreements with her uncle, Rubinstein moved to Melbourne, Australia, where she found work as a waitress, and then as a governess. In about 1902 or 1903, she opened her own beauty shop and sold a face cream that she had developed. As she built her business, she changed her name to Helena and asked to be addressed as Madame Helena Rubinstein. She also met and fell in love with Edward Titus, an American journalist. In 1908, Rubinstein went to

Polish immigrant Helena Rubinstein developed a face cream that launched a successful cosmetics enterprise. In time, the name Helena Rubinstein became synonymous with beauty.

London to learn more about skin care. Edward Titus joined Rubinstein in London and they soon married. The couple had two sons, Roy and Horace, born in 1909 and 1912, respectively. In their childhood, the boys went to boarding school, while Rubinstein expanded her business.

In 1915, the family moved to the United States to escape World War I. Rubinstein set up an upscale salon in New York City. Over the next two years, she also opened salons in other major cities. In addition, she trained sales women in department stores to sell the company's cosmetics.

Many businesses failed during the Great Depression, but Rubinstein's empire thrived, due in part to aggressive advertising that included portraits of her youthful sixty-year-old face. But her marriage was falling apart. Rubinstein divorced Titus in 1937. The next year, she married Georgian Prince Artchil Gourielli-Tchkonia, who was twenty years her junior.

Because of the prince's social connections, Rubinstein's enterprise attracted the world's most affluent people, and she became extremely wealthy. Although some people thought she was arrogant and haughty, Rubinstein contributed to numerous charities, and in 1953, founded the Helena Rubinstein Foundation. It supplied funds for medical research, health organizations, and art museums.

In 1955, Rubinstein's husband died of a heart attack, and by the 1960s, Helena's health was failing. Even then, she maintained control of her empire. She also wrote her autobiography, *My Life for Beauty*, which was published after her death on April 1, 1965. Since then, many writers and filmmakers have recounted the impact Rubinstein had on the beauty business: "She was said to have a cosmetics business worth somewhere between $17.5 million and $60 million, with international holdings, including laboratories, factories, and salons in fourteen countries."[10] Rubinstein's son, Roy, inherited the vast enterprise, and sold it within eight years. L'Oreal now owns the company.

ELIZABETH ARDEN (1881–1966)

Years before Rubinstein began to build her business in the United States, Elizabeth Arden had founded successful cosmetic enterprises in New York City and abroad. Arden and Rubinstein never met, but they were extremely competitive and bitter rivals for forty years.

Depending on the source, Elizabeth is said to have been born on December 31, 1876, 1878, 1881, or 1884, in Woodbridge, Ontario, Canada. "Birth records in Ontario confirm the 1881 date," according to history writer Patricia Daniels.[11] Elizabeth's actual birth name was Florence Nightingale Graham, after the famed English nurse Florence Nightingale. Her Scottish father, William Graham, and English mother, Susan Graham, were immigrants who married in Toronto and lived on a nearby farm. They had five children.

When Susan Graham became ill with tuberculosis, she asked a wealthy aunt to supplement the family's meager income, so that her children could be well educated. Because she could no longer care for the household, "Susan assigned chores to each of the children. Florence, who would become Elizabeth Arden in 1909, was to care for the family horse. In doing so, she developed a lifelong love of horses."[12] Hereafter, to avoid confusion, Florence will be called Elizabeth.

Susan Graham died of tuberculosis when Elizabeth was only six years old. The family was not only grief-stricken, but also faced financial problems. Susan's aunt no longer provided funds.

To help with finances, Elizabeth quit school and worked at various jobs. In 1908, she went to New York City to stay with her brother and look for work. She became a bookkeeper with the E. R. Squibb Pharmaceuticals Company. While there, she spent time in the labs and learned about skin care products. Later, she worked for Eleanor Adair, who had beauty salons in New York and Europe.

In 1910, Elizabeth set up her first shop. She named the salon after herself and painted the front door red. The door attracted attention and functioned as a logo for numerous Elizabeth Arden Red Door salons that followed in the United States and abroad. To increase her business, Arden created formulas for a variety of products, such as rouges and face powders, and in 1914, began to manufacture them. Apparently, over the next years, she found time for a romantic relationship, which resulted in marriage in 1918 to a US citizen, Thomas Lewis. With the marriage, Arden gained US citizenship.

Elizabeth Arden's popular salons and beauty products remain the gold standard in the industry today.

Lewis managed much of Arden's growing business, but his wife did not allow him to own stock in the company. The marriage began to fall apart when Arden discovered Lewis was unfaithful. The couple divorced in 1935. Five years later, Thomas went to work for Rubinstein.

Along with running her enterprise, she indulged in her longtime love for horses. She invested in several racing horse stables, hoping to add to her earnings. But many years passed before her horses paid dividends.

Arden expanded her enterprise by opening spas in the United States and Europe. During World War II, US government officials and others suspected that Arden's spas were hiding Nazi operations. However, the FBI investigated and found no evidence to support the allegations.

After the war, Arden continued to increase her business opportunities and cosmetic products. She advertised widely, and educated women on how to use makeup and maintain a youthful appearance.

Arden died on October 18, 1966. At the time, her enterprise included about one hundred salons. Eli Lilly bought the company in 1970, and it became part of a Unilever multinational corporation in 1990. In short, Florence Graham's modest beginning as an entrepreneur evolved because of her hard work and savvy business decisions. The result: Elizabeth Arden Company has had a long life even after Arden's death.

ESTÉE LAUDER (1908–2004)

Like her predecessors, Arden and Rubinstein, Estée Lauder began her cosmetic business in New York. At a young age, Estée developed a face cream and worked diligently to manufacture and sell it. She prospered and earned a fortune advertising and distributing cosmetics to women worldwide.

When Estée was born, her Jewish immigrant parents, Max and Rose Mentzer, of Queens, New York, named her Josephine Esther Mentzer and nicknamed her "Esty." Her birth date has been questioned. It is usually recorded as July 1, 1908, but some researchers say she was actually born in 1906 or 1907. Whatever the exact year, there is little doubt that she was interested in beauty treatments at an early age. Reportedly, she liked brushing her mother's long hair and applying her face cream. As a child, she also developed skills in merchandising while working in her father's hardware store.

Josephine learned how to make face cream from her uncle, John Shotz, a chemist who built a simple laboratory in a stable behind the Mentzer house. Her uncle encouraged Josephine to use the cream he had developed, rather than soap, on her face. She was so pleased with the cream that she convinced her classmates at Newtown High School in Queens to buy the product. Shotz's cream was the basis for the product that Josephine manufactured when she opened her cosmetic business. While a teenager, she sold her face cream to local beauty salons, calling the product "jars of hope."

When she was in her late teens, Estée met Joseph Lauter, a businessman of Austrian descent. The pair married on January 15, 1930, and not long afterward, changed their surname to Lauder, the original spelling. Three years later, they had a son, Leonard. Joseph managed the growing cosmetic business, but Estée was not happy in her role as homemaker and mother. In 1939, the couple divorced. But when their son became ill, they reunited and married again in 1941. Another son, Ronald, was born in 1943.

In spite of the turbulent marriage years, the couple created a company, and in 1946, the Lauders began operating as Estée Lauder Cosmetics Inc. The Lauders were the only personnel in the company, with Estée making just a few products in a building that once housed a restaurant. But the business expanded in 1947 and 1948, when Estée marketed and sold her cosmetics to the department store, Saks Fifth Avenue, and later, to Macy's, Bonwit Teller, Neiman Marcus, Marshall Field's, and others.

Throughout the 1950s, sales of Estée Lauder Cosmetics skyrocketed. A bath oil was added to the product line along with "a variety of other beauty aids, among them ... some 2,000 individual shades and items produced by five Lauder companies: Estée Lauder, Clinique, Origins, Prescriptives, and (for men) Aramis."[13]

The Lauders traveled widely and socialized with world leaders and US celebrities. They had homes in Manhattan and Long Island, New York; Palm Beach, Florida; France; and London.

Joseph Lauder died in 1983. Estée retired in 1995, and died in 2004. But her children and grandchildren have

Estée Lauder, shown here applying lipstick to a client, established a prestigious cosmetics empire that is still going strong seventy years later.

been involved in the business and can attest to the aptness of the title for Lauder's autobiography published in 1985: *Estée, A Success Story*. That success and multi-million-dollar enterprise continues to this day.

DAME ANITA PERILLI RODDICK (1942–2007)

Anita Roddick entered the beauty business for reasons quite different from those of Lauder, Arden, Rubenstein, and Walker. She was the founder of Body Shop, an international empire dedicated to

Dame Anita Roddick was an activist who wanted to create skin care and hair care prodcuts that would not harm animals or the environment. Consumers responded, and Roddick's Body Shop became a global empire.

social and environmental causes, and the sales of natural (nonchemical) soaps, creams, and lotions.

Born on October 23, 1942, she was named Anita Lucia Perilli by her Italian immigrant parents who owned a café in Littlehampton, England. As a child, she worked in the café that her mother, Gilda, operated. Her frugal mother saved empty containers and refilled them, a practice Anita followed later in her business.

Anita attended school at a convent, and then at a secondary school for girls. At the age of ten, she read a book about the holocaust, which awakened in her a "strong sense of moral outrage." She wrote: "I trained as a teacher but an educational opportunity on a kibbutz in Israel eventually turned into an extended working trip [representing the United Nations] around the world. Soon after I got back to England, my mother introduced me to a young Scotsman named Gordon Roddick. Our bond was instant. Together we opened first a restaurant, and then a hotel in Littlehampton."[14]

The Roddicks sold the restaurant in 1976 so that Gordon could follow a dream to ride a horse from Buenos Aires, Argentina, to New York. While her husband was gone, Anita had to earn a living and support the Roddicks' two daughters, Justine and Samantha (Sam). She opened the first Body Shop in the resort town of Brighton, England, to sell natural skin and hair care products. She explained that in her travels, she "had spent time in farming and fishing communities with pre-industrial peoples, and been exposed to body rituals of women from all over the world."[15] The products featured components made from fruits, seaweed, jojoba oil, elderflower extract, and other plant and herbal ingredients. She used refillable containers for her products and sold them at a low price. Along with her unique cosmetics, she included pamphlets about supporting people in developing countries by buying their products—"trade not aid," as it was called. She also publicly advocated for numerous environmental groups, and would not allow any products to be tested on animals.

Customers responded positively to Anita Roddick's activism. The Body Shop became so profitable that by the time Gordon returned from his trip in 1977, Anita had opened a second Body Shop store. In 1978, the Roddicks began selling Body Shop franchises. Over the next few years, and into the 1980s, they sold hundreds of Body Shop franchises in Europe and the United States. In 1984, the company went public—that is, sold shares to raise funds and grow the business. As the franchises spread worldwide along with the company's good works, Queen Elizabeth II appointed Anita Roddick a Dame Commander of the Order of the British Empire in 2003, honoring her distinguished service for charitable and welfare organizations. The appointment was one of many awards and honors Anita received during her business career.

In 2006, the French cosmetic corporation L'Oreal bought The Body Shop. The Roddicks trusted that L'Oreal would maintain their standards for Body Shop products. Anita Roddick stayed on as a consultant and member of the Board of Directors. But in 2007, she announced that she had hepatitis C, contracted from a contaminated blood transfusion years earlier. Her health deteriorated, and she died of a brain hemorrhage on September 10, 2007.

Eulogies came from around the world. British Prime Minister Gordon Brown (2007-2010) said of Dame Anita Roddick: "She campaigned for green issues for many years before it became fashionable to do so and inspired millions to the cause by bringing sustainable products to a mass market. As one of this country's most successful businesswomen, she was an inspiration to women throughout the country striving to set up and grow their own companies."[16]

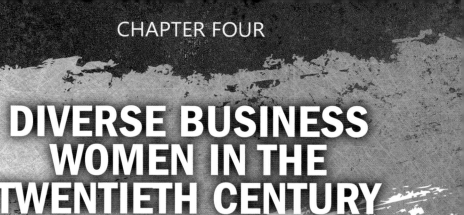

CHAPTER FOUR

DIVERSE BUSINESS WOMEN IN THE TWENTIETH CENTURY

During the twentieth century, there was no shortage of inventors, manufacturers, and business leaders. Together, they created and promoted a wide range of new products, such as adhesive bandages, airplanes, cotton swabs, popsicles, motorcars, and spray cans. Women were largely excluded from this world of business, which was still widely considered a male territory. Some women, however, were able to establish highly successful cosmetic and fashion businesses, as described in the previous chapter. Even so, most women were excluded not only from owning businesses, but also from waged work within them. In fact, at the beginning of the twentieth century, only 6 percent of married women worked outside the home—usually because their husbands were unemployed. Widowed and divorced women were in the workforce because they needed to earn an income.

In 1903, working women formed the National Women's Trade Union League to advocate for better wages and working conditions. Women also left their jobs in 1908 to strike and protest the sweatshop conditions in the factories where they worked. Soon after, many women worked to form a political party, the Congressional Union, which became the National Woman's Party, and published *The Suffragist* from 1913 to 1920, the year women won the right to vote.

World Wars I and II greatly altered women's "place" in society. With men in the armed services, women were needed to work in factories and public service jobs.

"Few areas of American life demonstrated such rapid and dramatic change during World War II as the social and economic roles of women," writes William H. Chafe, adding:

> Just a few months before Pearl Harbor, more than 80 percent of American men and women declared that it was wrong for wives to work outside the home if their husbands were employed. School systems throughout the country refused to hire women teachers if they were married, and fired them if they got married after being employed. Secretary of Labor Frances Perkins had denounced women as "pin money" workers for taking jobs away from needy men (the charge had no basis in fact), and the federal government itself prohibited by law the employment of two members

of the same family in the civil service. Now, suddenly, all that changed. Women workers became the secret weapons of democracy's arsenal, "Womanpower," the key to victory against fascism. Those who had been told just a few years earlier that they were threatening the nation's survival by taking jobs were now enjoined to rush to the workplace as part of their sacred patriotic duty.[1]

BREAKING BARRIERS

Even before women were employed for the war effort, they were sometimes able to break through into the "man's world." From the early 1900s on, women were, for example, mine owners, restaurateurs, television producers, newspaper publishers, and inventors.

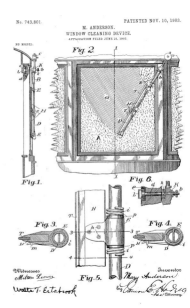

In 1903, rancher and real estate developer Mary Anderson (1866-1953) invented and patented the first automobile windshield wiper in Birmingham, Alabama. At first, auto manufacturers thought her invention was unnecessary. At the time,

This is the 1903 patent for Mary Anderson's "window cleaning device." Anderson's windshield wiper was an ingenious idea but failed to make it to production. Eventually, however, the wiper became standard in all automobiles.

drivers just opened a window and stuck their head out, to see where they were going when it was raining. After many attempts to manufacture the wiper, Anderson could not get any company to produce it. Her patent expired in 1920.

Hattie Carnegie (1880-1956), a US immigrant from Austria-Hungary, operated a highly successful enterprise as a fashion designer in New York City. In the 1920s, Paris designer Coco Chanel, mentioned earlier, found fame and fortune.

In 1922, sisters Clara (1886-1965) and Lillian (1884-1968) Westropp opened Women's Savings & Loan Company in Cleveland, Ohio. Operating with an all-female board of directors, they had a mission to educate women about money. The bank thrived, and by 1950, its assets exceeded $20 million.[2]

During the Great Depression of the 1930s, Hattie Austin-Moseley (1900-1998) was newly widowed, and needed to find a way to earn an income. In 1938, she opened Hattie's Chicken Shack in Saratoga Springs, New York, a horseracing mecca. Her southern-style food was so popular with racing fans that she was able to open a full-scale restaurant. As late as 2016, a restaurant with her name was still operating.

Margaret Rudkin (1897-1967) was another woman who became an entrepreneur during the Great Depression. Her family was affluent until the stock market crashed in 1929. At that point, she sold most of her property and belongings for funds. Also needing to treat her son's asthma and food allergies, Rudkin developed a recipe for a wheat bread that helped improve her son's health. She began to sell her bread, and eventually opened a successful business called Pepperidge Farm, which went on to produce cookies and other baked goods. Campbell Soup bought the company in 1961 for $20 million.

Other examples of early entrepreneurs include Ruth Wakefield, Olive Beech, Ruth Handler, and Diane von Furstenberg. Their profiles follow.

RUTH GRAVES WAKEFIELD (1903-1997)

Ruth Graves Wakefield invented the first chocolate chip cookie, the Toll House Chocolate Crunch Cookie, in 1938. Her combination of flour, sugar, butter, chocolate pieces, and nuts evolved into a business that grew rapidly and allowed Wakefield and her family an affluent lifestyle.

Born on June 17, 1903, in East Walpole, Massachusetts, she was named Ruth Graves by her parents, Fred and Helen Graves. It is not clear what happened to her mother, but when Ruth was twelve years old, her father remarried Harriette Ruggles Graves.

Little has been published about Ruth's early childhood and teen education, but records show that she attended Framingham State Normal School of Household Arts, a training school for teachers. She graduated in 1924 as a certified dietitian, and took a job as a home economics teacher at Brockton High School in Brockton, Massachusetts. She also worked as a hospital dietitian.

In 1926, Ruth married Kenneth Donald Wakefield. They had two children, Kenneth Donald Wakefield Jr. and Mary Jane Wakefield. In spite of the Depression, the Wakefields used their savings to buy a colonial-style house just outside Whitman, Massachusetts, in 1930. The building was said to be a toll house built in 1709. Toll houses were stops for stagecoaches along routes of travel. At these stops, passengers paid a toll (fee) for use of the route. Drivers also often took the opportunity to change horses, and travelers sought rest and a home-cooked meal in the house itself. Some stayed overnight.

Based on its storied history, the Wakefields turned their house into a lodge and restaurant and called it the Toll House Inn. Ruth prepared home-cooked meals and a variety of desserts that elicited rave reviews from her guests. The business grew as people came from all over New England to enjoy the food.

Ruth Wakefield's desserts included a variety of cookies based on colonial recipes. However, the chocolate chip cookie was a unique invention. Stories differ on how the concoction originated. One tale says that she accidentally developed the cookie by dropping squares of baker's bitter chocolate into a batter, expecting the squares to melt and create chocolate cookies. But Wakefield knew quite well that chocolate had to be melted (usually in a double boiler) before adding it to dough for a chocolate cookie.

Ruth Wakefield wisely negotiated for her Toll House Cookie recipe to be printed on packages of Nestlé chocolate chips.

Another origin story says that Wakefield planned to use a colonial recipe for Butter Drop Do cookies, but added pieces of semisweet chocolate bar to the mixture. But this recipe is actually a variation (no. 3) on gingerbread cake.[3] It is doubtful that Wakefield would have followed a cake recipe to create cookies.

Whatever her actual method, Wakefield developed a distinctive cookie, and successfully marketed it. She convinced the Nestlé Company to put her recipe on the back of their packages of chocolate chips, which helped her sell her product.

The Wakefields sold their restaurant in 1967. Although Ruth Wakefield was a successful entrepreneur, she did not talk about or publicize her achievements. Ruth Wakefield died on January 10, 1977. Her legacy is the Toll House Cookie, which speaks for itself in sales, and as it bakes in household ovens.

OLIVE ANN MELLOR BEECH (1903–1993)

Olive Beech was cofounder and president of Beech Aircraft Corporation of Kansas at a time in the nation's history when the aircraft industry was still in its early stages. Olive herself had no desire to pilot a plane, but she did have an early interest in running a manufacturing business. She had no qualms about being a female in a male-dominated enterprise.

Born on September 25, 1903, she was named Olive Ann by her parents Frank and Suzannah Mellor. Olive was the youngest of the four Mellor daughters. The family lived on a farm in Waverly, Kansas, but moved to Paola, Kansas, where Frank Mellor worked as a carpenter. In 1917, the Mellors moved again to Wichita, Kansas.

During her early childhood, Olive Ann showed

an aptitude for accounting. She had her own bank account at age seven, and by eleven, was handling the family accounts. Rather than attend high school, Olive opted to enroll at the American Secretarial and Business College in Wichita. When she was seventeen, she went to work as a book-keeper and office manager for a small company. A few years later, she was employed by the Travel Air Manufacturing Company, which was headed by Walter Beech. She was the only female employee. Even though she was "basically a shy person," she compensated with a "backbone of steel," noted Dennis Farney, author of *The Barnstormer and the Lady: Aviation Legends Walter and Olive Ann Beech*.[4]

Olive Ann learned all she could about the business. She handled company correspondence, records, and business transactions, and managed the office. Eventually, as the company grew, she became Beech's personal secretary. Olive Ann and Walter Beech married on February 24, 1930. They had two daughters, Suzanne, born in 1937, and Mary Lynn, born in 1940.

In 1932, in spite of the Depression, Olive and Walter each invested as co-owners of a company they named Beech Aircraft. Rather than manufacture an "affordable" plane, the company built a luxurious cabin biplane with staggered wings—that is, the top wing was set, or staggered, behind the bottom wing. Designed for wealthy businessmen, the plane became popularly known as the "staggerwing." At first, sales were slow. But sales accelerated after customers and pilots praised the deluxe interior and the plane's speed, which was faster than that of military planes.

Sales continued to increase for the company with the manufacture of Travel Air, the first plane with one set of wings. During World War II, Beech Aircraft produced planes for the military and expanded their workforce. In 1940, Walter Beech became seriously ill and was hospitalized. That same year, Olive was hospitalized to give birth to their second daughter, Mary Lynn. A company executive tried to take advantage of the couple's absence, and take over Beech Aircraft. Olive fired him along with other scheming employee.

Olive Ann Beech was not only unusual as a woman entrepreneur, she was a pioneer in aircraft manufacturing. Beech Aircraft was responsible for building luxury planes and military aircraft alike.

Walter was unable to return to work for months, and Olive managed the business. In 1950, Walter died suddenly of a heart attack. Olive Beech then became president of the company, which kept growing. Along with military aircraft, Beech sold products for space programs.

During Olive Beech's nearly two decades running the company, sales tripled.

While leading the company, Beech received numerous honors. For example, in 1970, *Fortune* magazine listed her as one of the ten highest-ranking women executives in major American corporations.

Beech Aircraft merged with the Raytheon Company in 1980, and two years later Beech retired. She died on July 6, 1993.

RUTH MOSCO HANDLER (1916–2002)

Many people may not recognize Ruth Handler's name, but they are likely to know the name of the doll she created: Barbie. Ruth and Elliot Handler along with Harold Matson founded the Mattel toy company during World War II and "by the mid-1940s, the young company [was] taking in revenues of $2 million (more than $26 million today)."[5]

Born on November 4, 1916 in Denver, Colorado, she was named Ruth Marianna Mosko. Her parents Jacob and Ida Mosko were Jewish immigrants from Poland and Ruth was the youngest of their ten children. After Ruth's birth, Ida was in poor health, so she sent her youngest daughter to live with her eldest daughter, Sarah, and her husband, Louie Greenwald. Ruth lived with them until she was nineteen. Sarah and her husband owned a drugstore and Ruth often worked there after her high school classes. She liked working and learning about business.

After graduating from high school, Ruth enrolled at the University of Denver. During her sophomore year, she vacationed in Los Angeles, California, and found a job at Paramount Studios. She stayed in California, and her high school boyfriend, Isadore "Izzy" Elliot Handler, soon joined her. In 1938, Ruth and Izzy married in Denver. They eventually had two children, Barbara (Barbie), born in 1941, and Kenneth (Ken), born in 1944.

When the couple returned to California, Ruth encouraged her husband to drop his nickname, "Izzy," and use his middle name, "Elliot." He enrolled in the Art Center College of Design while also holding a job as a designer of lighting fixtures. In addition, he began to design and then produce plastic accessories, which Ruth sold. They operated out of their garage at first, making miniature picture frames and then dollhouse furniture.

In 1945, the Handlers formed a partnership with Harold "Matt" Matson, and combined the letters in the men's names, "Matt" and "Elliot," to form "Mattel Creations." Matson soon became ill, and sold his share of the company to the Handlers.

Mattel began manufacturing toys. The first was a child-size plastic ukulele, called the "Uke-A-Doodle," introduced in 1947. The following year the company manufactured a plastic toy piano, which resulted in a net loss because it had to be redesigned due to quality problems.

In 1948, Mattel incorporated in California, and from 1950 to 1969, produced a great variety of toys, with sales reaching $14 million in 1958.

Ruth Handler cofounded Mattel, a wildly successful toy company that continues to manufacture the beloved and iconic Barbie doll.

Their sales soared in 1959, when Ruth Handler invented an adult-type fashion doll called Barbie, named after her daughter. Outfits for Barbie were manufactured and sold separately.

The doll was a hit with young girls, and fan clubs developed nationwide. Mattel produced Barbie's boyfriend Ken in 1961. Later, Mattel manufactured other dolls, including a baby doll that walked, and an African American doll. Other products included various activity toys, Hot Wheels miniature model cars (a huge success), and toys for boys, such as monster trucks and action figures. The company eventually became a major toy manufacturer with factories throughout the world.

In 1970, Ruth Handler discovered that she had breast cancer. After a mastectomy (surgical removal of the breast), she could not find a prosthesis—an artificial body part—that was satisfactory. So she created a company called Nearly Me to manufacture a device that was more like the human breast.

While Handler was ill, company executives mismanaged finances, prompting an investigation by federal authorities. Mattel and Ruth Handler were convicted of fraud, and Handler was forced out of the company. She adamantly and repeatedly denied any wrongdoing. Rather than go to trial, she accepted a sentence of community service and a hefty fine.

Ruth Handler died on April 27, 2002, due to complications from colon cancer. She is remembered for her essential role in inventing and marketing the Barbie doll and friends, which brought Mattel millions of dollars in annual revenue.

CHAPTER FIVE

SUCCESS DURING TURMOIL

After World War II, the United States enjoyed a thriving economy. In fact,"Between 1945 and 1960, the gross national product more than doubled, growing from $200 billion to more than $500 billion."[1] Economic prosperity, however, seemed to have little impact during the turmoil of the civil rights movement of the 1950s and 1960s.

The 1960s was also a time when the United States was embroiled in numerous crises: nuclear threats from Soviet missiles based in Cuba; assassinations of President John F. Kennedy, his brother, John Kennedy, and civil rights leader, Martin Luther King Jr. During the 1960s, protests against the Vietnam War also gathered steam. The marches and protests often became violent. The country was so divided by the US involvement in the war that the men and women who returned from the fighting were seldom given the honor and respect that veterans of other wars had received.

Other rebellions in the 1960s into the 1970s concerned women's rights. Increasingly, women of diverse ethnic backgrounds petitioned for their right to be employed in jobs traditionally held by men. Women also lobbied for laws that would allow them to obtain credit and borrow money to open businesses. Lenders at the time required that women have their husband or other male guarantee repayment of the loan. Women demanded that they be free of such restrictions.

With all the tragedy and travail in the United States, how could women hope to start businesses and create successful enterprises in the 1960s and 1970s? The National Women's History Museum, which has an exhibit online called "A Century of Entrepreneurial Women," explains:

> By the early 1960s, the changing social and cultural landscape provided new incentives for would-be women business owners. Divorce rates escalated during the 1960s and single mothers struggling to balance childrearing and their new roles as providers saw in business a possible solution ... [Women] started companies of their own as a way to assert their independence in the male world of business. When America's affluent decade of the '60s gave way to the recession of the 1970s, women who had worked their way into corporate America were often among the first to be let go. Many of them used their expertise to launch businesses of their own.[2]

Whatever the reasons for women becoming business owners, the stories of Brownie Wise, Joyce Chen, Jean Nidetch, and Lillian Vernon tell how they got started and became successful.

BROWNIE HUMPHREY WISE (1913–1992)

Brownie Wise brought plastic containers called Tupperware to national attention. She sold the products at house parties, where she demonstrated how they were used. Brownie was so successful that she became an executive for the Tupperware Company.

Born in 1913 in Buford, Georgia, she was named Brownie Mae Humphrey by her parents, Rosa Belle Stroud Humphrey and Jerome Humphrey, a plumber and hat maker. Rosa Belle and Jerome divorced when Brownie was still young. To make ends meet, Brownie's mother became a union organizer. Because her mother was often on the road, Brownie was sent to live with her Aunt Pearl, a dressmaker.[3]

Little is known about Brownie's early childhood or her education. From what we know, she attended school until the eighth grade—before leaving to be with her mother, and give speeches supporting unions in the South. She wanted to be a writer and illustrator, but she could only find employment in retail sales.

In 1936, Brownie met Robert Wise at the Texas Centennial Celebration, and the two eventually married. They moved to Detroit, Michigan, where Robert worked as a mechanic, and later set up a machine shop. Their only child, Jerry, was born in 1938. The couple's marriage fell apart and they divorced in 1941.[4]

To earn a living during the latter years of the Depression, Wise worked at several jobs. After the start of World War II, she got a job with Bendix Aviation Corporation. When the war ended, Brownie and her mother sold Stanley Home Products. Brownie's son, Jerry, became ill in 1949, and following a doctor's advice, the family moved to Miami, Florida. Brownie and her mother started a business called Patio Parties, selling household products, including Tupperware.

Earl Tupper was the inventor of Tupperware, unbreakable plastic bowls with patented covers that sealed tightly and did not leak. Tupper tried selling his containers at department stores, but had little success, primarily because customers needed to see how the seal lock worked. Tupper learned in 1950 that sales of his product at home parties were far better than at retail stores. In 1951, he created Tupperware Home Parties and hired Brownie Wise. She recruited and trained women to hold home parties and sell Tupperware, who then earned a percentage of the sales.

Brownie Wise didn't invent Tupperware, but she revolutionized the way it was sold. Wise's successful Tupperware parties inspired women to sell many different products simply by throwing a party at home.

Wise became well known across the nation, and stories about her and Tupperware appeared in numerous magazines and newspapers. She was the first woman to be featured on the cover of *Business Week*. Although sales of Tupperware soared across the nation, Earl Tupper resented Wise's celebrity. He fired her and sold his company in 1958.

Brownie Wise did not give up, and established another business to sell cosmetics at house parties.

The venture was not successful. She turned to consulting for direct sales companies. She also worked in real estate. Wise died in Kissimmee, Florida, in 1992.

"Although Brownie Wise's tenure as the head of a large corporation was brief, her impact was huge. Tupperware Home Parties became the gold standard for home party selling. Many other large companies, like Mary Kay Cosmetics, have copied the formula Wise perfected, extending her legacy in American business," noted PBS.[5]

JOYCE CHEN (1917–1994)

Joyce Chen popularized Mandarin Chinese food with her restaurants in Cambridge, Massachusetts, and also through her cookbooks and television show, *Joyce Chen Cooks*. She is known as well for the flat-bottomed wok that she invented.

Born in Shanghai (now Beijing), China, on September 14, 1917, Joyce Chen was the youngest of nine children. Chen's father was a well-paid government executive in China. He employed an excellent chef for his family, and often entertained his friends at home rather than at restaurants. Chen's childhood was filled with parties and food. When she was eighteen, she supervised a successful banquet, which prompted her interest in cooking.

Although they had a chef, Chen's mother also cooked, and urged her daughter to learn how to prepare food. Her mother told her that learning to cook would assure that she would not have to eat raw rice if she could not afford a family chef.

Joyce married Thomas Chen in 1943. When communists took over the Chinese government in 1949, Joyce, her husband, and their two children, Henry and Helen, boarded the last boat to leave Shanghai before the country's borders closed. A third child, Stephen, was born in the United States.

The Chen family settled in Cambridge, Massachusetts, and the children attended Buckingham School. In 1957, Joyce Chen made eggrolls for the school bazaar. The eggrolls were so popular they quickly sold out, and the school asked for more. At the same time, students from Shanghai studying at the Massachusetts Institute of Technology (MIT) were hungry for their home-style food. They urged Chen to open a restaurant, and loaned her money to help her get started.

In 1958, the Joyce Chen Restaurant opened. Many patrons had never sampled Mandarin-style cooking—foods from northern China. The restaurant offered these customers a choice between Mandarin and American dishes, both served in a buffet style. Chen also appealed to US diners by using English terms for Mandarin foods—referring to pot stickers, for example, as "Peking ravioli."

Chen opened three more restaurants in Cambridge, which were extremely popular.

Before the Food Network created celebrity chefs, Joyce Chen's TV show taught Americans about Mandarin cuisine.

According to her son, Stephen, president of Joyce Chen Foods, "she developed relationships with many well-known people," through these restuarants.[6] Celebrity chef Julia Child, former US Secretary of State Henry Kissinger, actor and singer Danny Kaye, and opera star Beverly Sills were among the famous patrons at Chen's restaurants.

In addition to establishing her restaurants, Chen also self-published the *Joyce Chen Cookbook*, which she sold to diners. Later, Lippincott commercially published the book in 1962. Her television show, *Joyce Chen Cooks,* was aired in 1967, and was the first national show that featured an Asian star. Chen also set up several companies, such as Joyce Chen Specialty Foods, and a company that sold cooking equipment, including the flat-bottom Peking Wok that she invented, patented, and marketed in 1970.

The enterprises boomed in the 1980s, but Joyce Chen suffered from Alzheimer's disease and had to be cared for in a nursing home. Her son, Stephen, took over the restaurant operations while the other children, Helen and Howard, managed the specialty foods and mail-order businesses. Joyce Chen died on August 23, 1994. Her legacy includes the continuing Chen enterprises and a Forever US postage stamp with Chen's portrait. The stamp was part of a 2014 series honoring five chefs who revolutionized cuisine in the United States.

JEAN SLUTSKY NIDETCH (1923–1915)

Jean Nidetch was determined to fight her obesity with a healthy weight-loss program. She turned that determination into a successful business as the founder of Weight Watchers International, which became a multimillion-dollar corporation. Nidetch changed the way people lose weight.

Born October 12, 1923 in Brooklyn, New York, she was named Jean Evelyn Slutsky by her parents David and Mae Rodin Slutsky. Her father drove a cab, and her mother was a manicurist. The family included Jean's younger sister, Helen. Both girls grew up in a household where food was often a remedy for whatever might be troubling them. Both Jean and Helen were chubby in their childhood, and struggled to control their weight. Jean tried a variety of diets and fasting, and would lose pounds, but gain it back again.

A student at Girls High School in Brooklyn, Jean graduated with a partial scholarship to Long Island

University. But her parents could not afford the additional tuition, so she enrolled at City College of New York, taking a course in business administration.

In 1942, Jean's father died, and she had to quit school and find a job. She worked for several companies until she found a job as a clerk at the Internal Revenue Service (IRS). While at the IRS, she met Mortimer "Marty" Nidetch. They married on April 20, 1947. The couple's first child died in infancy. A son, David, was born in 1952, and a second son, Richard, in 1956.

Marty Nidetch was a salesman for a blouse company in New York, and was promoted to a store manager position in Warren, Pennsylvania, in 1956. Within the year the family had moved back to New York, and Marty took a job as a bus driver. Jean Nidetch was a homemaker while the children were young, and was also a volunteer for various charities. At the same time, she was trying to control her weight, which did not feel healthy to her.

Nidetch went to the New York City Department of Health Obesity Clinic for help and received a strict diet. But she could not stick to it, and decided on a different course. She invited six friends who were also struggling with diets and weight loss, to meet at her home. They shared their experiences and recommendations from doctors and began to hold weekly, then bi-weekly, meetings to support each other and lose weight. As the meetings grew in participants, so did the publicity about the weight-loss methods, which included a nutritional, low-calorie diet and rewards for losing pounds. No alcohol, or sugary or high-fat foods were allowed.

In May 1963, she opened a business called Weight Watchers in the Little Neck region of Long Island. She had set up a corporation with Albert Lippert, a businessman, and his wife, Felice—a couple who had lost weight through Nidetch's program. They eventually formed a partnership. The enterprise grew rapidly, and by 1968, Weight Watchers franchises were operating nationwide.

Jean Nidetch turned her struggles with her weight into a successful business. Today, Weight Watchers helps people around the world get healthy.

Marty Nidetch did not like the changes in their lives, and the marriage ended in divorce in 1971. But Jean Nidetch continued with the enterprise she had founded. Throughout the 1970s the company expanded with worldwide franchises.

Nidetch was the spokesperson for Weight Watchers. She traveled extensively promoting the program. She also wrote several cookbooks and an autobiography published by the corporation. In 1973, she resigned as company president, and in 1978, H. J. Heinz Company bought Weight Watchers. Nidetch received more than $71 million for her share. She spent her later years in Florida, where her son David and her grandchildren lived. She died on April 29, 2015.

LILLIAN VERNON (1927–2015)

Lillian Vernon created a mail-order business that became well known across the United States. Her enterprise was the first female-owned business to be publicly listed on the New York Stock Exchange. A German-American, she is considered one of the most successful entrepreneurs of post-World War II history.

On March 18, 1927, Lilli Menasche—later known as Lillian Vernon—was born in Leipzig, Germany. Her father, Hermann Menasche, was a wealthy Jewish businessman and her mother, Erna, came from a family of diamond merchants in Belgium. Lilli and her older brother, Fred, were cared for and educated by nannies and governesses.

The family lived a privileged life, but after Hitler seized power in Germany, Hermann Menasche and his family fled to the Netherlands in 1935. Two years later they moved to New York City. Lilli, or Lillian, as she was called in America, was only ten years old, and had to adjust to a new country and language. The family lived in a German/Jewish neighborhood, but

Lillian's friends were primarily Americans because she found that was the easiest way to learn English and about US culture.

Lillian's parents did not adjust well to American life, and "the family never regained the status they had enjoyed in Germany. Hermann Menasche had hardly any knowledge of American business methods. He finally was moderately successful with a company manufacturing small leather goods like wallets, camera cases, and handbags. It was obligatory for the Menasche children to help out in their father's business on weekends, and their mother worked with her husband as well.[7]

Lillian's father regularly sent her into luxury shops to buy expensive leather handbags, which he copied and sold at lesser prices to department stores. The shopping experiences taught Lillian how to select items that were popular with buyers at lower prices. Despite playing this crucial role, her father never expected her to take over his business. As was the family custom, she was expected to marry, have children, and care for the household.

In 1946, she graduated from high school and enrolled in New York University. She later dropped out during her junior year, and married Sam Hochberg, who operated a dry goods store in Mt. Vernon, New York. The couple had two sons, Fred, born in 1952, and David, born in 1956.

Trained by her father as a young girl, Lillian Vernon learned how to select merchandise that consumers wanted to buy. Long before the popularity of online shopping, Vernon's mail-order catalog allowed people to purchase from home.

To help out with the family income while tend-
ing to her household, Lillian Hochberg had started a
mail-order business in 1951, working from her home.
She named the business Vernon Specialties, and spe-
cialized in low-cost, monogrammed handbags, belts,
and other items. As the business grew, Sam Hochberg
became unhappy with Lillian's ambition to be a successful entrepreneur. In 1969, the couple divorced.

Lillian remarried, but this second marriage
also ended in divorce. Her third husband, Paolo
Martino had no part in the Lillian Vernon
Corporation. The enterprise had enlarged its
catalog to sell household goods, a lady's tool
kit, luggage, and many other items. Vernon sold
her corporation in 2003 for $60.5 million to
Ripplewood Holdings, but served as honorary
chairwoman until 2006. When Lillian Vernon
died on December 14, 2015, the *New York Times*
obituary noted: "Ms. Vernon was a role model
for many women in business. She had started her
company at a time when working mothers were
often criticized ... and as a female entrepreneur
she had overcome obstacles in getting credit from
skeptical banks."[8]

CHAPTER SIX

CONTEMPORARY WOMEN ENTREPRENEURS

I n the US business world today, female entrepreneurs are not as harshly criticized as their forerunners of earlier times. However, business was especially difficult for everyone during the recession years between 2002 and 2007. After that, as the economy picked up, hundreds of new women-owned firms started each day.

Personal computers, printers, and other electronics have helped many women begin home businesses that have grown from humble operations into sophisticated, high-earning enterprises. Women have also received help from the Office of Women's Business Ownership (OWBO), which is an agency of the US Small Business Administration. The OWBO offers a number of programs that provide business training and counseling, access to credit and capital, and marketing opportunities to women entrepreneurs.

Sometimes necessity or frustration drives potential women entrepreneurs to take steps to market products, services, or inventions. Consider Erin Balogh, the mother of two young girls in 2009. She worked full-time as an emergency room nurse. While getting ready for work, she was often frustrated because there was no safe space in her small bathroom with its pedestal sink for her curling iron or flat iron. After numerous experiments, she invented a heat resistant silicon holder that was the prototype for the Hot Iron Holster now sold across the United States. As she invented new merchandise, she recruited her husband to run daily operations and manage the company's new product development.

Another example is Melissa Kieling, a single mom with three children. She had to pack lunches for the children to take to school. But she puzzled over how to keep the lunches cool and safe. She patented a lunch bag with a built-in freezable gel. Her invention became the PackIt Personal Cooler, and within five years, was a $14 million business.[1]

THE STATE OF WOMEN IN BUSINESS

The *2015 State Of Women-Owned Businesses Report* (the latest publication) contains numerous statistics on women entrepreneurs. Much of the information is based on US Census data. The report indicates that the number of women-owned firms has continued to increase since its first annual publication in 2011. However, the women-owned businesses are "smaller than the average firm."

According to the report, the number of US women-owned firms is now estimated to be more than 9.4 million enterprises—30 percent of all businesses in the country. These companies employ more than 7.9 million workers and generate "nearly $1.5 trillion in revenues ...Women-owned business are found in all sectors of the economy," but the largest number "is in health care and social assistance." The report also notes that women-owned businesses include, but are not limited to, trade, finance, technical/scientific services, auto repair, construction, real estate, education, and food services.

Minority women—African American, Asian American, Latina, Native American/Alaska Native, Native Hawaiian/Pacific Islander—who own businesses were charted in the report. Data show they have gained considerably in numbers. In 1997, minority women owned almost one million firms. But, says the report, "That number has skyrocketed to an estimated 3,111,300 as of 2015."[2]

Vickie Wessel, of Cherokee, Choctaw, and Apache descent, is just one example. She is the president of Spirit Electronics based in Phoenix, Arizona. The company has been in operation since 1979. "Wessel's company distributes semiconductors, capacitors, resistors, connectors—anything that gets manufactured onto a circuit board that goes into some type of electronics. That includes communications equipment, missile guidance systems, and satellites. Her customers are some of the biggest government contractors, including Raytheon, Lockheed, Boeing, General Dynamics, and Northrop Grumman."[3]

As women increasingly start or expand businesses, they receive support from numerous groups and funders that help women with business start-ups. Today, entrepreneurship is no longer considered a "man's world." In other words, women have been able to break through many barriers. Successful contemporary women entrepreneurs like Diane von Furstenberg, Arianna Huffington, Oprah Winfrey, Weili Dai, and Nely Galan, are both an indication of this progress, and a force in its continuation, as they inspire women today to pursue their dreams.

DIANE VON FURSTENBERG (1946–)

She is a fashion designer famous for her signature wrap dress made of clinging jersey material, which was widely popular in the 1970s and again in the 1990s. Diane von Furstenberg is an entrepreneur whose products now include a variety of attire, shoes, handbags, accessories, eyewear, jewelry, rugs, household items, cosmetics, and books she has written.

Diane was born on December 31, 1946, in Brussels, Belgium, and her name at birth was Diane Simone Michelle Halfin. Her parents were Leon Halfin, a successful Romanian businessman, and Liliane Nahmias Halfin, a Holocaust survivor. As Diane tells it:

> When my mother was 20, she was a prisoner of war and went to Auschwitz. She was there for 13 months … But she survived. She weighed 49 pounds … And when she came back to Belgium, she married my father. They said to her: "You can't have a child. It won't be normal, you won't survive." And I was born nine months later. That is my flag."[4]

Growing up in a privileged household, Diane's education took place in several nations: Switzerland, Spain, and England. She attended the University of Geneva (Switzerland) in 1965, where she met Prince Eduard Egon von

Fürstenberg, known as Egon. After college, Diane worked for a fashion photographer's agent in Paris, France, and also for a textile manufacturer in Italy, where she designed some silk jersey dresses.

Diane and Egon married in 1969, and she became Diane Prinzessin zu Fürstenberg. Their children include a son, Alexandre, and a daughter, Tatiana. Diane wanted to maintain her independence, so with the prince's support, she opened a studio in Italy, creating designs for knit dresses. Egon, meanwhile, was living in New York City and training for a position at Chase Manhattan Bank. Diane joined him in New York, and they led a luxurious, flamboyant life. During their marriage, Egon was often unfaithful. The couple separated in 1973, divorcing ten years later. Diane kept the last name, and her products became known by her initials, DVF.

In 1974, DVF introduced the wrap dress to the world. It was and is designed for

Diane von Furstenberg created the now-iconic wrap dress, a revolutionary uniform of sorts for the growing ranks of working women.

the mass market rather than elite fashion buyers. With women's increasing role in the workplace, the dress was appropriate for the office as well as for evening wear. DVF soon had a profitable business. By 1976, she had sold 5 million wrap dresses. Stories about her and her design appeared in major publications.

Diane continued to attend parties and dated numerous celebrities. At one party in 1974, she met Barry Diller, a billionaire media tycoon. They became friends, lovers, and eventually, they married.

By the early 1980s, DVF dresses had reached their limit in potential customers, and von Furstenberg faced bankruptcy. She went to Europe and began a French publishing house. She also sold a line of clothing on a home shopping network. In the early 1990s, she returned to the United States and wrote books that described and illustrated the decorative homes of celebrities.

In the late 1990s, von Furstenberg revived the wrap dress with an above-the-knee hemline. The shorter version resurrected the DVF business, and today, the apparel sells worldwide. Although she enjoys her success, Diane von Furstenberg has also made philanthropy an important part of her life. In her view, someone who is privileged has a duty to give back. Her life today involves work with numerous non-profit organizations and the Diller-von Furstenberg Family Foundation. It honors women who have displayed leadership, strength, and courage in their commitment to their causes. She is also a board member of Vital Voices, an international organization that empowers emerging female leaders and social entrepreneurs worldwide.

ARIANNA HUFFINGTON (1950–)

Millions of readers know her because of her online magazine *The Huffington Post*. Arianna Huffington is also well known as a television personality, political pundit, and international media tycoon.

Huffington was born on July 15, 1950, in Athens, Greece, to Konstantinos and Elli Stassinopoulos. Arianna was the first of two daughters. Her younger sister is Agapi.

Konstantinos Stassinopoulos was a newspaper publisher who survived a Nazi concentration camp during World War II. This experience affected him for the rest of his life. "He had the survivor's mentality," Huffington told *Vanity Fair*. "In his case, it was 'I can do whatever. The rules don't apply to me.'"[5] He started newspapers that failed and went bankrupt. He had "endless affairs," Arianna said. When Arianna was still in

Greek primary school (ages six to twelve), her parents divorced.

Elli was the parent who had the most influence on Arianna's upbringing and education. "My mother instilled in me that failure was not something to be afraid of, that it was not the opposite of success. It was a steppingstone to success. So I had no fear of failure. Perseverance is everything. I don't give up. Everybody has failures, but successful people keep on going," Arianna told Mary Vinnedge.[6]

Arianna's mother encouraged her daughter to go to Girton College, Cambridge, even though Arianna knew little English, and Elli had to scramble for funds to pay the tuition. When she was sixteen, Arianna moved to the United Kingdom. At Cambridge, she was on the debate team, which was a dominating force in her life. She earned a master's degree in economics, graduating in 1972. While in college, she met and fell in love with Bernard Levin. Unfortunately, Levin did not want marriage and children, as Arianna did.

After graduation, Arianna worked as a columnist, critic, and television host. Her first book, *The Female Woman*, published in 1973, became a bestseller and brought her much recognition. Since then, she has authored more than a dozen books, including biographies of famed artist, Picasso, and opera star, Maria Callas.

Arianna Huffington launched a website, *The Huffington Post*, in 2005. The award-winning site quickly grew to become a global influence in the realm of politics and beyond.

In 1980, Huffington moved to New York City with her mother. She quickly established herself in celebrity social circles, and in September, 1985, met and dated Michael Huffington, heir to a Texas oil fortune. Six months later, on April 12, 1986, they married. Their daughter, Christina, was born in 1989, and their daughter, Isabella, in 1991.

The Huffingtons moved to Santa Barbara, California, where Michael Huffington ran and was elected to a seat as a US Congressman, serving from 1993-1995. He also ran for the US Senate in 1992, but lost to incumbent Diane Feinstein. The Huffingtons divorced in 1997.

Arianna Huffington ran for governor of California in 2003, challenging Arnold Schwarzenegger on the Independent ticket. She withdrew from the campaign, however, to work against the recall of then-Governor Gray Davis, who was eventually forced out of office. Huffington continued her political activism, espousing conservative views at first, but later supporting liberal causes. In 2005, she launched her website, *The Huffington Post*, which soon became one of the most popular sites for American and global politics, and won a Pulitzer Prize.

In 2011, AOL bought *The Huffington Post* for $315 million, and formed The Huffington Post Media Group, with Arianna Huffington as its president and editor-in-chief. Huffington's media empire has continually expanded over the years. In 2015, *Forbes* magazine named Arianna Huffington one of the world's 100 most powerful women.

In 2016, Arianna Huffington announced that she was leaving the *The Huffington Post* to focus on her new company, Thrive Global. This wellness business will help people reduce stress and exhaustion while pursuing a successful career.

OPRAH WINFREY (1954–)

Most Americans and people worldwide know her name. Oprah Winfrey is a powerful media entrepreneur, TV host, actress, and producer. She is one of America's wealthiest women, named by *Forbes* in 2007 as the world's only black billionaire.

Oprah Winfrey was born on January 29, 1954, in Kosciusko, Mississippi. Oprah's parents, who were not married, are Vernon Winfrey and Vernita Lee. She was given the biblical name Orpah, which is on her birth certificate, but no one could pronounce it, so she was called Oprah.

When Oprah's parents separated, Vernita Lee, like many other black people migrating north, went to Milwaukee, Wisconsin, to work as a housemaid. Oprah was sent to live on a farm with her grandmother, Hattie Mae Lee. During her childhood, Oprah had few material things, but her grandmother taught her to read and write when she was just two or three years old. She often recited Bible verses and gave speeches in church.

Oprah received her first dress and shoes when she went to school, starting in first grade and soon skipping to third grade. Her life changed dramatically in 1960. At six years old, she went to live with her mother in an inner city Milwaukee neighborhood, where she was sexually abused by male relatives and friends of her mother. At the age of twelve, Oprah's mother sent her to Nashville, Tennessee, to live with her father, who had strict standards. For a short time, she thrived with her father's help. But her mother wanted her to return to Milwaukee, and as an adolescent, she became involved in drugs, got pregnant, and lost a premature baby. She was yet again sent to her father, whom she credits with saving her life by providing strict guidance and loving care.

After graduating from high school, she attended Tennessee State University with a full scholarship, majoring in speech and drama. During her sophomore year, she became the news anchor on Nashville's television station. She graduated in 1976, and accepted an offer to be a co-anchor of the six o'clock news on WJZ-TV in Baltimore, Maryland. Later, she became a host of the station's local talk show, *People Are Talking*. She was with WJZ-TV for seven years before she moved to Chicago, Illinois, in January of 1984. She anchored *A.M. Chicago*, a morning talk show emphasizing current and controversial issues. In September of 1985, the program became *The Oprah Winfrey Show*, and later, part of Winfrey's Harpo Productions, which produced her show until 2011.

Oprah has never married, but has had a long-time relationship with Stedman Graham, an educator and businessman. Over the years, Oprah Winfrey has had one success after another. She starred in the 1985 film *The Color Purple*, produced a TV miniseries in 1989 and 1990, and launched *"Oprah's Book Club,"* a TV talk show for book discussions, in 1996. She went on to produce and star

Few men or women enjoy the mass influence that Oprah Winfrey does. Having reigned supreme in the media world for decades, Winfrey is considered one of the world's most accomplished and admired people living today.

in the 1998 film *Beloved*, began publication of *O, the Oprah Magazine* in 2002, and has written both books and articles. She is also a generous contributor to numerous causes, awarding over four hundred scholarships to historic black Morehouse College. In 2013, she was awarded the Presidential Medal of Freedom, the nation's highest civilian award recognizing exceptional service to the country.

In 2015, Winfrey, who has struggled most of her life with weight issues, invested $43.2 million in Weight Watchers and began its diet plan. She lost twenty-six pounds and celebrated with photos in *O Magazine's* April 2016 issue.

It would require hundreds of pages to document in detail all of Oprah Winfrey's accomplishments. But to put it simply, she has inspired millions to overcome obstacles, improve their lives, care for others, and realize their dreams.

WEILI DAI (1961–)

Weili Dai is the cofounder and president of Marvell Technology Group Ltd., which makes semi-conductors. The company has at least seven thousand employees and ships more than one billion chips a year to customers such as Microsoft, Hewlett-Packard, and IBM. In 2015,

Forbes magazine listed Dai as one of America's Richest Self-Made Women.

Born in 1961 in Shanghai, China, Weili Dai's exact date of birth is unclear. She was educated in China, and while in school, played basketball from aged nine to fourteen. She is passionate about basketball, and was on a semi-professional team. She credits the sport as being "the foundation for everything ...When you do math, you have to think fast and have creativity, and basketball required that. A lot of energy too ... And teamwork is absolutely key. For us to win the championship, it's not one superstar–it requires five. It's team work, encouragement, positive attitude, confidence," she told a *Forbes* staff interviewer.[7]

In 1979, Dai emigrated from China with her family to San Francisco, California, where she finished high school. After graduation she enrolled

Weili Dai is a founder of Marvell Technology Group, a successful manufacturer of semiconductors.

at the University of California, Berkeley, and earned a Bachelor's Degree in computer science. She met Sehat Sutardja, an electrical engineering student, at the university. Later they married and had two sons.

For a time, following college graduation, Dai worked as a software developer. After Sutardja earned his doctorate, he and Weili Dai co-founded Marvell (short for marvelous) Technology Group Ltd. in 1995. Based in Santa Clara, California, Marvell manufactures semiconductors, basic components for electronics. Semiconductors are used to produce chips for electronic devices, such as computers, cell phones, iPods, and BlackBerries.

Since its beginning, Dai has been the guiding force in Marvell's success. It has become one of the top semiconductor companies in the world. Dai has held various positions in the company, and became president of Marvell in 2013. She was appointed to the company's board in 2014. Sehat Sutardja is CEO of the company.

As sales of electronics and the wireless devices grew, so did Marvell's revenue, which is now in the billions of dollars. Dai and Sutardja have shared their wealth with contributions to technology and society. Dai leads Marvell's global civic engagements and the company's partnership with the One Laptop Per Child program (OLPC). The program's mission is to provide one connected laptop

CONTEMPORARY WOMEN ENTREPRENEURS

for every school-age child in developing countries in order to aid their education.

Dai mentors women starting new technology firms while she and her husband continue their almost non-stop roles in philanthropy and entrepreneurship. She believes there is still much to do in her field and that technology education should start in the early grades, and through high school. As she put it, "Let students use technologies in the classroom. And we can make Barbie more high-tech, with some robotic function."[8]

NELY GALÁN (1963–)

Nely Galán is a first generation Latina immigrant and self-made media mogul. She is a former president of the US television network *Telemundo,* and has produced hundreds of TV episodes in Spanish and English. Since 1994, she has also owned and operated her own media company. *The New York Times Magazine* called her the "Tropical Tycoon."

Born in Santa Clara, Cuba, on January 1, 1963, she was named Arnely Álvarez by her parents, Arsenio and Nelinda. Her parents combined their names to create Arnely. She hated the name, so she shortened it to "Nely."

When she was two years old, Nely and her parents immigrated to Teaneck, New Jersey.

Bright and ambitious, Nely Galán strove to become an entrepreneur from an early age. She launched the *Telemundo* network in 1994.

While she was growing up, businesswomen were her models and heroines. On her bedroom wall, "she hung a photo of Sherry Lansing, the first woman to head a Hollywood studio."[9]

Nely attended a Catholic high school for girls and was a good student. While in high school she wrote a satire titled "Why you should not send your daughter to an all-girl Catholic High School." She submitted the piece to *Seventeen* magazine. The magazine's editors were so impressed that they published her essay and asked her to be a guest editor. As a result of her article, she was expelled from school. But she "fought back under the 1st Amendment," she said in an interview, "and the nuns took me back, graduated me early and I was able to do the guest editorship at *Seventeen Magazine*. It taught me that authority isn't always right and it doesn't pay to be a wimp and take it. You have to fight back and sometimes you will win."[10] She later became a full-time editor at the magazine's New York office.

When she was eighteen, Nely married Hector Galán, a documentary filmmaker. They divorced four years later. She then pursued her goal of becoming an entrepreneur. When she was twenty-two, she became a manager at New York's WNJU TV. From that station she was able to launch the *Telemundo* network. Since 1994, she has operated her own company, Galán Entertainment, based in Venice, California. The firm focuses on Latino programming at Fox TV.

In 2012, Galán founded the Adelante Movement (*adelante* in Spanish means "forward"). Galán explains that it "is a digital platform and national tour ... I am on a Coca-Cola advisory board, and they told me that Latinas were the emerging market and the fastest growing entrepreneurs. When I heard that, I felt that at this point in my life, what could be more important than creating a private sector approach to creating economic opportunities for the women in my community, which, in turn, would change the economics of the Latino family ... My goal is to train 30,000 Latinas by the year 2020, and to create an entrepreneurial business in the home of every Latina going forward. I am a woman that believes in ownership and entrepreneurship as the way for most women to have financial freedom and become actualized."[11]

CONCLUSION: THE BOTTOM LINE

In business, the bottom line, or the income left after paying expenses, determines whether an enterprise will succeed or fail. For many women entrepreneurs, however, there is another bottom line: smashing the barriers—breaking the invisible glass ceilings that prevent women from achieving their business goals. Since colonial days, those barriers have slowly fallen. From merchant and ship owner Margaret Hardenbroek De Vries Philipse of the 1600s to media mogul Nely Galán of today, women have proven they can defy convention and be successful entrepreneurs. As *Forbes* contributor Geri Stengel noted: "What's good for women is good for the economy. Economists and academics agree women entrepreneurs are an under-tapped force that can rekindle economic expansion."[12]

Sallie Krawcheck, CEO of a digital investment company, forecast that 2016 would be "The Golden Age of Female Entrepreneurship." She predicted the year and beyond would bring together "the forces of entrepreneurialism and feminism ... Together, they will drive a long-wave, golden age of female entrepreneurship, which will be a positive for all of us: positive and empowering for the women who make the leap, good for the economy, good for consumers, and good for society."[13]

CHAPTER NOTES

CHAPTER 1. BEFORE AND AFTER THE REVOLUTION

1. "Margaret Hardenbroek De Vries Philipse," The National Society of Colonial Dames in the State of New York, http://www.nscdny. org/major-projects/margaret-hardenbroek/ (accessed March 25, 2016).
2. Jean Zimmerman, *Women of the House: How a Colonial She-Merchant Built a Mansion, a Fortune, and a Dynasty* (Orlando, FL: Harvest Books/ Harcourt, 2007), paperback edition, p. 50.
3. Maggie MacLean, "Margaret Hardenbroeck Philipse," womenhistoryblog.com, February 1, 2008, http://www.womenhistoryblog. com/2008/02/margaret-hardenbroeck-philipse. html (accessed January 29, 2016).
4. Elizabeth D. Schafer, "Alexander, Mary Spratt Provoost Merchant," American History Online, September 22, 2015, http://www. worldhistory.biz/modern-history/81881-alexan- der-mary-spratt-provoost-1693-1760-merchant. html (accessed January 30, 2016).
5. Women's Project of New Jersey, Joan N. Burstyn, ed. *Past and Promise: Lives of New Jersey Women* (Syracuse University Press, 1997; first published in 1990 by Scarecrow Press, Metuchen, NJ), p. 6.
6. Mbaldock, "Fabric Samples from an Early New

York Businesswoman," nyhistory.org, March 4, 2011, http://www.nyhistory.org/fabric-samples-early-new-york-businesswoman (accessed January 30, 2016).

7. National Women's History Museum, "Mary Katherine Goddard (1738-1816)," https://www.nwhm.org/education-resources/biography/biographies/mary-katherine-goddard/ (accessed February 3, 2016).

8. Francis J. Walet, *Patriots, Loyalists and Printers* (Worcester, Mass: American Antiquarian Society, 1976), p. 88.

9. Ed Crews, "The Truth about Betsy Ross," *Colonial Williamsburg Journal*, Summer 2008, http://www.history.org/Foundation/journal/Summer08/betsy.cfm (accessed February 3, 2016).

CHAPTER 2. STRIVING AMIDST WARS

1. Center for Lowell History, University of Massachusetts Lowell Library, Mary Cowles letter to her sister, December 6, 1847, http://library.uml.edu/clh/All/cow.htm (accessed February 5, 2016).

2. Thomas Dublin, "Women and the Early Industrial Revolution in the United States," gilderlehrman.org, n.d., https://www.gilderlehrman.org/history-by-era/jackson-lincoln/essays/women-and-early-industrial-revolution-united-states (accessed February 6, 2016).

3. Martha J. Coston. *A Signal Success: The Work and Travels of Mrs. Martha J. Coston. An Autobiography*. Philadelphia, PA: J.P. Lippincott, 1896 (public domain digital copy), p. 10.

4. Ibid., p. 38.

5. "Night Signals," Signal Corps Association, http://www.civilwarsignals.org/pages/signal/signalpages/flare/coston.html (accessed February 9, 2016).

6. Denise E. Pilato, "Martha Coston: A Woman, a War, and a Signal to the World," civilwarsignals.org, n.d., http://www.civilwarsignals.org/pages/signal/signalpages/flare/coston2.html (accessed February 12, 2016).

7. Sarasota County Government, "Bertha Honore Palmer—the Manatee County Years," scgov.net, n.d., https://www.scgov.net/BerthaPalmer/Pages/About.aspx (accessed February 12, 2016).

8. James M. Manheim, "Maggie Lena Walker (1867?-1934)," Contemporary Black Biography, 1998, encyclopedia.com, http://www.encyclopedia.com/topic/Maggie_Lena_Walker.aspx#1 (accessed February 14, 2016).

9. National Park Service, "Who Was Maggie Lena Walker?" nps.gov, n.d., http://www.nps.gov/mawa/learn/historyculture/index.htm (accessed February 14, 2016).

CHAPTER 3. WOMEN IN BEAUTY AND FASHION BUSINESSES

1. Public Broadcasting Service, "The Works Progress Administration," pbs.org, n.d., http://www.pbs.org/wgbh/americanexperience/features/general-article/dustbowl-wpa/ (accessed February 15, 2016).

2. Ibid.

3. "Rosie the Riveter," History.com, http://www.history.com/topics/world-war-ii/rosie-the-riveter (accessed April 21, 2016).

4. Regina Blaszczyk in Smithsonian Institution, "Women in Business: A Historical Perspective," amhistory.si.edu, 2002, http://amhistory.si.edu/archives/WIB-tour/historical.pdf (accessed February 16, 2016).

5. Sean Silverthorne, "The History of Beauty," (interview with Professor Geoffrey Jones, Harvard Business School), April 19, 2010, http://hbswk.hbs.edu/item/the-history-of-beauty (accessed February 15, 2016).

6. Henry Louis Gates, Jr., "Madam Walker, the First Black American Woman to Be a Self-Made Millionaire," pbs.org, n.d., http://www.pbs.org/wnet/african-americans-many-rivers-to-cross/history/100-amazing-facts/madam-walker-the-first-black-american-woman-to-be-a-self-made-millionaire.

7. Martha Lagase, "HBS Cases: Beauty Entrepreneur Madam Walker," hbswk.hbs. edu, June 25, 2007, http://hbswk.hbs.edu/item/ hbs-cases-beauty-entrepreneur-madam-walker (accessed February 18, 2016).

8. Lindy Woodhead, *War Paint: Madame Helena Rubinstein and Miss Elizabeth Arden, Their Lives, Their Times, Their Rivalry* (Hoboken, NJ: John Wiley and Sons, 2004), p. 20.

9. Sara Alpern, "Helena Rubinstein," Jewish Women's Archive, jwa.org, n.d., http://jwa. org/encyclopedia/article/rubinstein-helena (accessed February 19, 2016).

10. Ibid.

11. Patricia Daniels, "Who Was Elizabeth Arden?" history1900s.about.com, updated September 26, 2014, http://history1900s.about.com/od/ people/fl/Elizabeth-Arden.htm (accessed February 22, 2016).

12. Ibid.

13. Richard Severo, "Estée Lauder, Pursuer of Beauty and Cosmetics Titan, Dies at 97," *The New York Times*, April 26, 2004, http://www.nytimes. com/2004/04/26/nyregion/estee-lauder-pursu- er-of-beauty-and-cosmetics-titan-dies-at-97. html?_r=0 (accessed February 24, 2016).

14. Dame Anita Roddick, "About Dame Anita Roddick," anitaroddick.com, n.d., http://www.

anitaroddick.com/aboutanita.php (accessed February 26, 2016).

15. Ibid.

16. "Dame Anita Roddick," thebodyshop.com, http://www.thebodyshop.com/services/aboutus_anita-roddick.aspx (accessed January 22, 2016).

CHAPTER 4. DIVERSE BUSINESS WOMEN IN THE TWENTIETH CENTURY

1. William H. Chafe, *William H. "World War II as a Pivotal Experience for American Women," In Women and War: The Changing Status of American Women from the 1930s to the 1940s*, edited by Maria Diedrich and Dorothea Fischer-Hornung (New York: Berg, 1990), pp. 21-34.

2. The Encyclopedia of Cleveland History, "Women's Federal Savings Bank," http://ech.case.edu/ech-cgi/article.pl?id=WFSB (accessed February 29, 2016).

3. Amelia Simmons, American Cookery, http://www.gutenberg.org/cache/epub/12815/pg12815-images.html (accessed March 2, 2016).

4. C-Span, "Book Discussion on The Barnstormer and the Lady," c-span.org, May 10, 2012, http://www.c-span.org/video/?306274-1/book-discussion-barnstormer-lady (accessed March 5, 2016).

5. Public Broadcasting service, "Ruth Handler," pbs.org, n.d., http://www.pbs.org/wgbh/theymadeamerica/whomade/handler_hi.html (accessed March 7, 2016).

CHAPTER 5. SUCCESS DURING TURMOIL

1. "The 1950s," History.com, http://www.history.com/topics/1950s (accessed March 13, 2016).
2. National Women's History Museum, "1960–1979 America's New Social Reality: the 1960s," entrepreneurs.nwhm.org, n.d., http://entrepreneurs.nwhm.org/#/1960-1979/1 (accessed March 14, 2016).
3. Public Broadcasting Service, American Experience, "Brownie Wise," pbs.org, n.d., http://www.pbs.org/wgbh/americanexperience/features/biography/tupperware-wise/ (accessed March 14, 2016).
4. Mimi Minnick, "Brownie Wise Papers, ca 1928-1968," amhistory.si.edu, revised December 20, 2001, http://amhistory.si.edu/archives/d7509.htm (accessed March 15, 2016).
5. Public Broadcasting Service.
6. Stephen Chen, "Chef. Restaurateur. Entrepreneur.," joychenfoods.com, September 26, 2014, http://joycechenfoods.com/about/legacy (accessed March 17, 2016).
7. Ute Mehnert, "Lillian Vernon (1927-2015),"

immigrantentrepreneurship.org, updated
December 21, 2015, http://www.immigranten-
trepreneurship.org/entry.php?rec=72 (accessed
March 19, 2016).

8. Lynn Povich, "Lillian Vernon, Creator of a
Bustling Catalog Business, Dies at 88," *The
New York Times*, December 14, 2015, http://
www.nytimes.com/2015/12/15/business/
lillian-vernon-creator-of-a-bustling-catalog-
business-dies-at-88.html?_r=0 (accessed March
14, 2016).

CHAPTER 6. CONTEMPORARY WOMEN ENTREPRENEURS

1. Kate Taylor, "10 Single Mom Entrepreneurs
Share Their Best Business Advice," entre-
preneur.com, August 2, 2015, http://www.
entrepreneur.com/slideshow/239018 (accessed
March 19, 2016).

2. "Amex State Of Women-Owned Businesses
Report," http://www.womenable.com/content/
userfiles/Amex_OPEN_State_of_WOBs_2015_
Executive_Report_finalsm.pdf (accessed March
20, 2016).

3. Christopher Geoffrey McPherson, "Spirit
Electronics President Broke the Gender
Barrier in Business," azcentral.com, June 17,
2015, http://www.azcentral.com/story/money/

business/2015/06/17/whos-who-2015-vickie-wessel/71261042/ (accessed March 28, 2016).

4. Philip Galanes, "The Director David O. Russell and the Designer Diane von Furstenberg Discuss the Creative Process in Film and Fashion," *The New York Times*, February 7, 2014, http://www.nytimes.com/2014/02/09/fashion/David-O-Russell-Diane-von-Furstenberg.html?ref=dianevonfurstenberg&_r=2 (accessed March 9, 2016).

5. Suzanna Andrews, "Arianna Calling!" *Vanity Fair*, October 17, 2006, http://www.vanityfair.com/news/2005/12/huffington200512 (accessed March 22, 2016).

6. Mary Vinnedge, "Arianna Huffington: Pushing the Limits," success.com, September 19, 2010, http://www.success.com/article/arianna-huff-ington-pushing-the-limits (accessed March 21, 2016).

7. Jeanna Goudreau, "With Bartz Out, Marvell's Weili Dai Pushes Women In Tech," *Forbes*, September 13, 2011 http://www.forbes.com/sites/jennagoudreau/2011/09/13/bartz-out-yahoo-marvell-weili-dai-women-in-tech-xerox-apple-cisco/print/ (accessed March 26, 2016).

8. Ibid.

9. Samantha Cole, "Meet the Woman Inspiring Thousands of American Latina Entrepreneurs,"

fastcompany.com, March 15, 2014, http://www.fastcompany.com/3043672/strong-female-lead/meet-the-woman-inspiring-thousands-of-american-latina-entrepreneurs (accessed March 27, 2016).

10. Dr. Vrunda Davé, "Break the Glass Ceiling: A Conversation with Nely Galan," nelygalan.com, February 2015, http://www.nelygalan.com/wp-content/uploads/2015/02/Savvy-Biz-Women-Feb-2015.pdf (accessed March 27, 2016).

11. David J. Parnell, "Media Mogul Nely Galan, On Succeeding Through Diversity," *Forbes*, March 13, 2015, http://www.forbes.com/sites/davidparnell/2015/03/13/media-mogul-nely-galan-on-succeeding-through-diversity/2/#62887bc61ecd (accessed March 23, 2016).

12. Geri Stengel, "Why the Force Will Be with Women Entrepreneurs in 2016," *Forbes*, January 6, 2016, http://www.forbes.com/sites/geristengel/2016/01/06/why-the-force-will-be-with-women-entrepreneurs-in-2016/#108085e84ce2 (accessed March 28, 2016).

13. Sallie Krawcheck, "We're Entering the Golden Age of Female Entrepreneurship—and It'll Be Amazing," linkedin.com, December 14, 2015, https://www.linkedin.com/pulse/big-idea-2016-were-entering-golden-age-female-itll-sallie-krawcheck (accessed March 21, 2016).

abolitionists People opposed to and fighting against slavery.

almanac An annual book with weather forecasts, records of farmers' planting dates, tide tables, and other information.

apprentice A person learning a trade or skill from an experienced individual.

boilerplates Steel plates to cover the hulls of ships.

circa Approximately or about, particularly concerning dates.

commission A payment for a service or product sold.

crepe Silk, cotton, or other crinkled, lightweight material.

indigenous people The peoples living in a region prior to colonization.

fascism A right-wing, nationalistic, and authoritarian ideology or governmental system.

forfeit Give up or lose.

gold fever A term for the excitement during the rush to find gold between 1840 and 1850.

Great Depression The US economic crisis of the 1930s.

Manifest Destiny A belief that Americans had the divine right to possess the entire North American continent.

menstruation A natural discharge of blood and tissue from the uterus, usually occurring monthly in post-pubescent females with uteruses.

militia Citizen soldiers.

Northwest Territory A region made up of the land that is now known as Ohio, Indiana, Illinois, Michigan, Wisconsin, and the eastern part of Minnesota.

opulent Very rich or luxurious.

Parliament The legislative body (lawmakers) in Great Britain.

patent An inventor's or creator's exclusive right to manufacture or sell a product or service.

pleurisy A lung disease.

submissive Inclined or expected to be obedient, or to comply to others' wishes.

upholstery Padded covering on furniture.

FURTHER READING

BOOKS

Albee, Sarah. *Why'd They Wear That?: Fashion as the Mirror of History*. Des Moines, IA: National Geographic Children's Books, 2015.

Bundles, A'Llia. *Madame Walker Theatre Center: An Indianapolis Treasure*. Charleston, SC: Arcadia Publishing, 2013.

Kealing, Bob. *Life of the Party: The Remarkable Story of How Brownie Wise Built, and Lost, a Tupperware Party*. New York, NY: Crown Archetype, 2016.

Lacey, Robert. *Model Woman: Eileen Ford and the Business of Beauty*. New York, NY: HarperCollins, 2015.

Mariotti, Steve. *The Young Entrepreneur's Guide to Starting and Running a Business: Turn Your Ideas into Money!* New York, NY: Crown, 2014.

Richard, Doug. *How to Start a Creative Business: The Jargon-Free Guide For Creative Entrepreneurs* Newton Abbot, Devon, UK: David and Charles, 2013.

Winfrey, Oprah. *What I Know For Sure*. New York, NY: Flatiron Books, 2014.

WEBSITES

National Park Service
www.nps.gov/
Describes national parks, historical sites, and
important people in US history.

National Women's History Museum
www.nwhm.org/
Contains information about prominent women
in American history.

Signal Corps Association
www.civilwarsignals.org
Describes how naval signal flares work.

Women History Blog
womenhistoryblog.com
Presents biographies of colonial women,
women of the American Revolution, and
nineteenth-century women.

INDEX

H

Handler, Ruth Mosco,
71–74
Homespun Movement, 10
Hot Iron Holster, 91
Huffington, Arianna,
97–100
Huffington Post, The , 97, 100

I

Independent Order of St.
Luke (IOSL), 39–40
Industrial Revolution, 44

J

Joyce Chen Cookbook, 82
Joyce Chen Cooks, 82

K

Kieling, Melissa, 91

L

Lauder, Estée, 55–57
Lauter, Joseph, 56–57
Lilly, Eli, 54
L'Oreal, 51, 60
Lukens, Rebecca, 23–24
Lydia E. Pinkham's
Vegetable Compound,
28, 30–31

M

Madam Walker's
Wonderful Hair
Grower, 47
mail-order business, 89
Mandarin cuisine, 81
Manifest Destiny, 27
Marvell Technology Group,
104, 106–107
Mary Kay Cosmetics, 80
Maryland Journal, 18–19
Massachusetts Institute of
Technology, 81
Mattel, 72–74
Mecom, Jane, 9
My Life for Beauty, 51

N

National Association for
the Advancement
of Colored People
(NAACP), 40, 48
National Women's Party, 62
National Women's Trade
Union League, 62
Nestlé Company, 68–69
New Amsterdam, 11–14
Nidetch, Jean Slutsky, 83–86

O

Oprah's Book Club, 103
Oprah Winfrey Show, The, 102
O, the Oprah Magazine, 104